Effective Program Models
for Gifted Students From
Underserved
Populations

Effective Program Models
for Gifted Students From
Underserved
Populations

Edited by

Cheryll Adams, Ph.D., and
Kimberley Chandler, Ph.D.

A CEC-TAG Educational Resource

Cheryll M. Adams, Ph.D., Tracy L. Cross, Ph.D., Susan K. Johnsen, Ph.D., and Diane Montgomery, Ph.D., Series Editors

PRUFROCK PRESS INC.
WACO, TEXAS

Library of Congress Cataloging-in-Publication Data

Effective program models for gifted students from underserved populations : edited by Cheryll M. Adams, Ph.D., and Kimberley L. Chandler, Ph.D.
    pages cm
ISBN 978-1-61821-096-8 (pbk.)
1. Gifted children--Education--United States. 2. Children with social disabilities--Education--United States. I. Adams, Cheryll M., 1948-
LC3993.9.E39 2013
371.95--dc23
                              2013019066

Edited by Rachel Taliaferro

Cover and layout design by Raquel Trevino

ISBN-13: 978-1-61821-096-8

Printed in the United States of America.

At the time of this book's publication, all facts and figures cited are the most current available. All telephone numbers, addresses, and websites URLs are accurate and active. All publications, organizations, websites, and other resources exist as described in the book, and all have been verified. The editors and Prufrock Press Inc. make no warranty or guarantee concerning the information and materials given out by organizations or content found at websites, and we are not responsible for any changes that occur after this book's publication. If you find an error, please contact Prufrock Press Inc.

Prufrock Press Inc.
P.O. Box 8813
Waco, TX 76714-8813
Phone: (800) 998-2208
Fax: (800) 240-0333
http://www.prufrock.com

Table of Contents

Introduction

This publication provides coordinators, teachers, administrators, parents, and other interested parties with information about effective program models for underserved gifted students. In this book, we identify eight successful programs that have been designed to use with low-income, high-ability students. Each chapter includes an introduction and brief overview of the model, how students are identified for the program, which talents are valued, the goals of the project, a description of the model, difficult issues and how they are addressed, important contributions of the program, research findings, how the program is sustained, and contact information.

Two entries focus specifically on primary-aged students: Young Scholars and Project Clarion. Young Scholars is a model for finding and nurturing potential in diverse populations of young students; it started in one large district and has been replicated in various sites across the country. Project Clarion was a Javits demonstration project that focused on developing and nurturing science talent in primary students. An interesting connection is that the curriculum units developed in Project Clarion are frequently used as a component of some Young Scholars programs.

Project Athena and Project M³ (Mentoring Mathematical Minds) were Javits demonstration projects that were developed to nurture students in the upper elementary grades. Project Athena was a language arts program that used curriculum originally designed specifically for gifted students in a heterogeneous, Title I setting in which there were often no identified students. Project products included novel study guides to give teachers additional options and a program for scaffolding reading comprehension. Project M³ was also a program that generated curriculum products, but with an emphasis on identifying and nurturing math talent.

The chapters on Project Nexus, the Next Generation Venture Fund, Project EXCITE, and the TEAK Fellowship describe programs that provide support in various ways and in differing degrees for secondary students. Although the Project Nexus program and Project EXCITE were funded through public monies, the Next Generation Venture Fund and the TEAK fellowship were dependent on private and corporate sponsorships.

By including models and programs that span the grade levels, focus on different content areas, and represent a variety of funding schemes, it is hoped that the reader will be able to understand the diverse options that have been implemented effectively in finding and nurturing students from underrepresented populations. Although it may not be possible to replicate a given program exactly in one's own district, the detailed description and the inclusion of contact information should give an administrator a starting point for developing a program tailored to his or her context.

chapter 1

Project EXCITE

Kourtney Cockrell

Introduction

Project EXCITE is a collaborative project involving Northwestern University's School of Education and Social Policy through its Center for Talent Development (CTD), Evanston/Skokie School District 65, and Evanston Township High School District (ETHS) 202. Although African-American and Latino students comprise approximately 50% of students at Evanston Township High School, they are underrepresented in advanced mathematics and science classes, comprising only 18% of the students enrolled at the AP level and 21% at the honors level. Project EXCITE addresses the achievement gap in the Evanston schools by providing supplemental educational opportunities for minority students demonstrating potential for high achievement in math and science. The primary goal of EXCITE is to prepare its students to be successful in honors and AP courses when they transition to high school.

In 1998, in collaboration with teachers from ETHS, the Center for Talent Development at Northwestern University began development of Project EXCITE. The first cohort of Project EXCITE was a group of third graders selected during the 2000–2001 school year. During each subsequent year, Project EXCITE has continued to select a cohort of 20–25 underrepresented third-grade students from five participating District 65 elementary schools. EXCITE currently serves approximately 150 underrepresented minority students in grades 3–8.

Project EXCITE is a 6-year program that provides an array of supports and services to minority students, including enrichment classes held after school, on weekends, and during the summer; tutoring; practice and preparation for important "gateway" exams for math and high school placement; and educational guidance and counseling. Students receive support through this program until they begin high school, when they enter other existing programs for minority students that continue to support them academically in ETHS (e.g., Steps Toward Academic Excellence [STAE], and Advancement by Individual Determination [AVID]).

Selection Process

Project EXCITE works closely with its partner schools to select a new cohort of third-grade students each year. The process begins in the fall of third grade with an open invitation to all parents of African American and Latino students, regardless of family income level. Parents receive this information from their child's third-grade teacher and are encouraged to register for the EXCITE selection process. The registration process involves two steps: signing up to take two standardized, norm-referenced tests—the Iowa Tests of Basic Skills (ITBS; Hoover, Dunbar, & Frisbie, 2001) and the Naglieri Nonverbal Ability Test (NNAT; Naglieri, 1995)—and submitting a teacher recommendation form. Students are tested in groups of 20–25 children on two Saturday mornings in the fall.

Project EXCITE students are selected based on their potential to achieve at high levels as demonstrated by their ability to think critically and engage in problem solving, as well as by a high level of interest, curiosity, and enthusiasm for learning mathematics and science as communicated on their teacher recommendation forms. Selection is also based on positive work habits, previous achievement, and ability. Specifically, students must score at or above the 75th percentile on a reading or math subtest of the Iowa Tests of Basic Skills and/or at or above a stanine of six on the Naglieri Nonverbal Ability Test. Project EXCITE students are selected without regard to family income, as research suggests that educational disparities between underrepresented minorities and White students exist at every socioeconomic level—including those at the very top.

Project EXCITE Goals

The general long-range goal of Project EXCITE is to close the gap in academic achievement between minority and majority students by bolstering the achievement and success of gifted minority children. The specific long-term goal is to increase the number of minority students enrolling and succeeding in the advanced and honors math and science programs at ETHS. Currently, EXCITE is pursuing the following immediate goals to achieve the general and specific long-term goals: (a) the identification of African-American and Latino children in early elementary school (by third grade) with talent and ability in mathematics and science; (b) the provision of supplemental educational opportunities to ensure that selected students complete algebra and have a significant science laboratory experience by the end of eighth grade; (c) increased support for high achievement and talent development through significant and sustained interactions with older student role models and with teachers and other adults; (d) the cultivation of a positive peer culture by encouraging the formation of a supportive group of peer and family participants; and (e) the development of a strong community of families who can support one another and build relationships.

Project EXCITE Program Components

There are three primary components of Project EXCITE aimed at addressing its goals and objectives. These components include academic enrichment, parent education and support, and supplemental programming and resources.

Academic Enrichment

Project EXCITE's 6-year program model provides participants with excellent instruction in mathematics and the sciences and the chance to bond with like-minded students. Through completing more than 400 hours of supplemental education experiences and by developing a network of supportive friends, Project EXCITE participants transition to high school with the confidence and the ability to excel in the most challenging honors and AP courses. Students who have been accepted into the program participate in various activities during each year of the 6-year sequence. All academic activities are mandatory with the exception of summer programs offered before sixth grade.

Beginning in third grade, Project EXCITE students participate in academic enrichment activities consisting of integrated math and science experiments. These activities take place after school at their local high school. Students in third grade may also take enrichment classes during the summer. Students in grades 4, 5, and 6 take classes on Saturdays through the CTD's Saturday Enrichment Program (SEP). These consist of two 8-week sessions of Saturday classes in the fall and winter. SEP is designed to offer enriching and challenging courses to students from preschool to ninth grade. The SEP program allows students to explore various areas of science, mathematics, humanities, and the fine arts. In fourth grade, Project EXCITE students are grouped together for some special Saturday classes to promote friendships and connections between Project EXCITE students who come from five different schools.

Beginning in fifth grade, students choose a math or science class from the courses offered in the SEP program. The fifth-grade

SEP experience allows students the opportunity to begin developing friendships with other gifted students from across the Chicago area, while exploring their interests in math and science. Students in grade 5 are invited to participate in a summer reading program hosted by Evanston Public Library. In sixth grade, Project EXCITE students are grouped together again in a special Saturday class to focus on pre-algebra as well as to develop critical study and organizational skills that are essential for succeeding in middle school. During the summer after sixth grade, students participate in Apogee, the summer program for students completing grades 4 through 6, at the Center for Talent Development. Summer classes are enriching in nature in the areas of language arts, science, mathematics, social science, and the fine arts. Project EXCITE students can choose either a math or science summer course. The summer Apogee experience fosters creativity, independence, and confidence in its students by allowing them to explore a topic in detail while learning from other gifted students who come from across the country and even the world.

Students in grades 7 and 8 take an SEP course in math or science during the winter. During the summer after grade 7, students participate in a 3-week science program at ETHS that features one week each of biology, chemistry, and physics. These students gain a significant lab experience through participation in the program. The final academic enrichment opportunity provided to EXCITE students is the summer bridge program that takes place after graduation from eighth grade. The bridge program is designed to give EXCITE students a head start on coursework that they will take their freshman year and to get them familiar with the high school environment. Students cover advanced math concepts (Geometry/Algebra II) and apply what they learn by focusing on physics-related projects. The program also focuses on reading comprehension as it relates to biology and the sciences in general.

Parent Education and Support

Project EXCITE provides comprehensive support to its parents and families. Up to two family meetings are held each year for each grade level (grades 3 to 8). Family meetings serve as an opportunity for families to connect with one another, set expectations for the year, and hear from guest speakers about important topics in the world of gifted education. Speakers focus on the ways in which parents can cultivate high achievement and work with schools to ensure that students are performing at high levels in school. Parents are also invited to attend parent workshops and seminars organized by the Center for Talent Development during the Saturday Enrichment Program. The Excite Project Coordinator meets with parents on occasion to address concerns about individual children. Recently, Project EXCITE introduced two new resources that focus on education and support for parents. The EXCITE Parent Committee was launched in Spring 2012 in order to strengthen the Project EXCITE community through family socials and outings, as well as to provide parent education in the form of workshops that address psychosocial needs of gifted minority students. In addition, Project EXCITE partners with Northwestern University's Family Institute to provide free therapy sessions to parents seeking guidance around social or emotional challenges that their child may be experiencing.

Supplemental Programming and Resources

In an effort to ensure comprehensive and individualized support to EXCITE students, free tutoring services are provided to students in middle and high school. Students are matched one-on-one with a Northwestern undergraduate or graduate student to receive homework help and test prep support. Middle and high school students are also encouraged to volunteer with Project EXCITE. Students can provide administrative support at family meetings, volunteer with younger students in elementary school during the afterschool program, and gain hands-on classroom experience during the summers as teacher assistants.

Things to Consider When Serving Underrepresented Gifted Learners

The experiences of underrepresented gifted children within the context of their schools, families, and communities are complex and vary greatly by individual, family, and school context. The following four topics have proven to be particularly relevant for Project EXCITE students and families: (a) cultural awareness and competency; (b) parenting and family dynamics; (c) peer groups; and (d) psychosocial needs and mindsets.

Building Cultural Awareness and Competency

Identifying underrepresented students and placing them into gifted programs and activities are just the beginning of a multi-faceted process. Gifted programs and academic institutions must be prepared to invest resources, time, and training toward creating more inclusive and culturally competent curriculum and instruction. Ford (2011) suggested that in order for underrepresented gifted students to demonstrate the necessary motivation, effort, and attitude needed to become high achievers, the educational environment must include culturally responsive curriculum in all subject areas, recruit and retain racially and culturally diverse teachers, and integrate multicultural education into the educational process rather than relating it superficially to the core curriculum as an add-on.

Project EXCITE staff are involved at all levels of program development in order to ensure a positive experience and academic outcome for its students. As an example, EXCITE staff sit on hiring committees and help to facilitate diversity trainings for staff and teachers each year. Additionally, EXCITE staff work closely with families to ensure they are supported and prepared to be successful before programs begin each quarter.

The Power of Parents and Family Support

Project EXCITE families defy the stereotype of low-income, minority parents as being uninvolved with their children and not stressing or valuing education. EXCITE parents are extremely supportive of their children's ambitions and dreams and most directly support their academic careers. These observations are consistent with the findings of researchers such as Clark (1983) and Sampson (2002), who have studied this topic and found common themes around parenting high-achieving minority students, which include having high expectations for their children and being assertive in their children's education. Educators need to find ways of involving parents in developing positive parent-child relations that are nurturing, supportive, respectful, and open. Project EXCITE's family meetings, the new parent committee, and the recent partnership with the Family Institute work in tandem to ensure that this critical parent-child dynamic is maintained, cultivated, and supported.

Cultivating Peer Group Support

Peer groups have also been shown to impact the long-term success of underrepresented gifted children. Ford (2011) and Hébert (2011) have studied this topic in detail and found that these students tend to engage in supportive social networks that include high-achieving peers and friends who want to succeed academically and can provide emotional support and encouragement to each other. In culturally diverse environments similar to the community in which Project EXCITE exists, Ford (2011) cautioned that loneliness and isolation are of special concern for Black students when they are severely underrepresented in gifted programs. Project EXCITE works to build a strong network within and across each cohort by bringing students together in class during grades 4 and 6 and by providing opportunities for students to engage informally during family socials and special field trips.

Psychosocial Needs and Mindsets Matter

Over the past decade, a number of researchers have presented new perspectives and theories about the psychological factors involved in mindsets, motivation, and achievement (Subotnik, Robinson, Callahan, & Gubbins, 2012). Aronson and Juarez (2012) and Good (2012) presented evidence that these psychological constructs can significantly affect the achievement of underrepresented groups and can be particularly damaging to high-performing minority students who are typically more invested in doing well than their lower-performing or average peers (Dweck, 2012). Stereotype threat research suggests that students underperform in environments when their identity is associated with a negative stereotype because they worry about confirming that stereotype (Aronson & Juarez, 2012). In these environments, students experience disruptive levels of anxiety, which in turn interferes with their ability to think well and focus. Aronson and Juarez (2012) also found that teaching Dweck's (2006) growth mindset to underrepresented minority students could help to mitigate stereotype threat. However, they found that for some students, holding a strong fixed mindset was sometimes beneficial for gifted minority students, as these students had a strong academic self-concept and the confidence to take on increasingly challenging academic experiences. Good (2012) posited that the level in which students feel connected to or accepted into various academic domains can impact student achievement and performance. Good suggested "a lack of belonging may include feeling out of place, undervalued, uncomfortable, unaccepted, mistrustful of the academic environment, and ultimately, can result in students exhibiting an inability to truly engage with one's academic world" (p. 40). Project EXCITE staff report that their middle school students begin to struggle with issues of motivation, confidence, and mindsets primarily in seventh and eighth grades and as they transition to high school. As such, determining how to best support these needs will become increasingly important for the long-term success of Project EXCITE students.

Important Contributions & Research Findings

One of the most promising aspects of Project EXCITE is that it embodies a growing area of research in the world of gifted education by focusing more on talent development rather than on traditional conceptions of giftedness. Historically, giftedness has been thought to be a genetic or inherited trait (Subotnik, Olszewski-Kubilius, & Worrell, 2012). However, a growing body of research suggests that

> "Giftedness can be viewed as developmental in that in the beginning stages, potential is the key variable; in later stages, achievement is the measure of giftedness; and in fully developed talents, eminence is the basis on which this label is granted. Both cognitive and psychosocial variables play an essential role in the manifestation of giftedness at every developmental stage, are malleable, and need to be deliberately cultivated." (Subotnik et al., 2012, p. 7)

Project EXCITE fully embraces this definition by expanding its selection criteria in order to identify and cultivate the rich potential that so many young children possess. Project EXCITE students are selected based on scoring at or above the 75th percentile on the Iowa Tests of Basic Skills or at or above a stanine of six on the Naglieri Nonverbal Ability Test. Once admitted into the EXCITE program, these students thrive and excel in a number of CTD programs and activities with other gifted students who scored at or above the 95th percentile on nationally normed-referenced tests. This demonstrates the significance and value in broadening traditional admissions criteria in order to provide access and opportunity to students from all racial and economic backgrounds. It also diminishes the significance of test scores as sole predictors of future achievement and success.

Another compelling argument for the support of program models like Project EXCITE are the substantial outcomes that EXCITE students have demonstrated. It appears that EXCITE students close the achievement gap in their community (Evanston, IL) by grade 8 based on their scores on the Illinois Standard Achievement Test (ISAT). EXCITE students enter fourth grade scoring just 6 points above the average score for African American and Latino students in the district, well below that of White students who are the highest achieving group in the district. However, by eighth grade, EXCITE students have made significant gains, enabling them to score at levels comparable to White students in the district. Additionally, 70% of EXCITE students enter high school having completed one or more years of high school math, higher than the district average of 50% across all students, putting them on track to complete BC Calculus by their senior year. The Project EXCITE model represents the importance and power of outside-of-school programming for students via partnerships between local schools and institutions of higher education. Often, colleges and universities are situated in close proximity to areas that have high rates of poverty and could benefit from outside-of-school enrichment programming (Columbia University in Harlem, New York City; Johns Hopkins University in Baltimore, MD; Northwestern University in Evanston, IL; University of Chicago in Hyde Park, Chicago; University of Southern California in Compton, CA; and Yale University in New Haven, CT). The resources and expertise that institutions of higher education can provide to low-income and minority communities are invaluable and will help this nation move one step closer to narrowing its growing income and education divide.

Program Funding and Contact Information

Project EXCITE is primarily funded by Northwestern University with a small portion of the budget covered through the local school districts in Evanston, Districts 65 and 202.

For more information, contact:

Kourtney Cockrell
Project EXCITE Coordinator
k-cockrell@northwestern.edu.

References

Aronson, J., & Juarez, L. (2012). Growth mindsets in the laboratory and the real world. In R. F. Subotnik, A. Robinson, C. M. Callahan, & E. J. Gubbins (Eds.), *Malleable minds: Translating insights from psychology and neuroscience to gifted education* (pp. 19–36). Storrs: University of Connecticut, The National Research Center on the Gifted and Talented.

Clark, R. (1983). *Family life and school achievement: Why poor black children succeed and fail.* Chicago, IL: University of Chicago Press.

Dweck, C. (2006). *Mindset: The new psychology of success.* New York: Ballantine Books.

Dweck, C. (2012). Mindsets and malleable minds: Implications for giftedness and talent. In R. F. Subotnik, A. Robinson, C. M. Callahan, & E. J. Gubbins (Eds.), *Malleable minds: Translating insights from psychology and neuroscience to gifted education* (pp. 7–18). Storrs: University of Connecticut, The National Research Center on the Gifted and Talented.

Ford, D. Y. (2011). *Multicultural gifted education* (2nd ed.). Waco, TX: Prufrock Press.

Good, C. (2012). Reformulating the talent equation: Implications for gifted students' sense of belonging. In R. F. Subotnik, A. Robinson, C. M. Callahan, & E. J. Gubbins (Eds.), *Malleable minds: Translating insights from psychology and neuroscience to gifted education* (pp. 37–54). Storrs: University of Connecticut, The National Research Center on the Gifted and Talented.

Hébert, T. P. (2011). *Understanding the social and emotional lives of gifted students.* Waco, TX: Prufrock Press.

Hoover, H., Dunbar, S., & Frisbie, D. (2001). *Iowa Tests of Basic Skills* (Form A, Level 9). Itaska, IL: Riverside.

Naglieri, J. (1995). *Naglieri Nonverbal Ability Test.* San Antonio, TX: Harcourt Brace.

Sampson, W. A. (2002). *Black student achievement: How much do family and school really matter?* Lanham, MD: Rowman & Littlefield.

Subotnik, R. F., Olszewski-Kubilius, P., & Worrell, F. C. (2012). A proposed direction forward for gifted education based on psychological science. *Gifted Child Quarterly, 56,* 176–188.

Subotnik, R. F., Robinson, A., Callahan, C. M., & Gubbins, E. J. (Eds.). (2012). *Malleable minds: Translating insights from psychology and neuroscience to gifted education.* Storrs: University of Connecticut, The National Research Center on the Gifted and Talented.

chapter 2

Project *M³*
Mentoring Mathematical Minds

M. Katherine Gavin

Introduction

More than 30 years ago, the National Council of Teachers of Mathematics (NCTM, 1980) in their *Agenda for Action* stated, "The student most neglected in terms of realizing full potential is the gifted student of mathematics. Outstanding mathematical ability is a precious societal resource, sorely needed to maintain leadership in a technological world" (p. 18). It is unfortunate that not much has changed over the years. Both at the international and national levels, it is embarrassing to report the small numbers of U.S. students who score at the advanced level. In the most recent Trends in International Mathematics and Science Study (TIMSS, 2008), only 6% of our eighth graders and 10% of our fourth graders achieved that benchmark, whereas more than 40% of students in Singapore and other Asian countries scored at the advanced level. On the National Assessment of Educational Progress (NAEP, 2011), only 7% of fourth graders and 8% of U.S. eighth graders reached the advanced level. The numbers get worse as researchers disaggregate the data to examine students by race/ethnicity and socioeconomic status (SES). Of fourth graders, only 4% of students receiving subsidized lunch scored at the advanced level, while a meager 1% of Black students and 2% of Hispanic students achieved this status. At the eighth-grade level, 5% of students receiving subsidized lunch, 2% of Black students, and 3% of Hispanic students reached this benchmark. Clearly, educators are continuing to neglect our students with mathematical talent and talent potential. It was in recognition of this deficiency and in hopes of identifying and nurturing math talent in students, especially those at risk who frequently go unnoticed, that Project M³: Mentoring Mathematical Minds was conceived.

Project M³ Goals

In 2002, we received a five-year U.S. Department of Education Jacob K. Javits curriculum and research grant to fund Project M³. The overall goal of the project was to help mathematically promising elementary students learn and enjoy more complex mathematics and achieve at internationally competitive levels. In order to accomplish this goal, we realized that we must identify more traditionally underserved students including economically disadvantaged, limited English proficient, and minority students for the math talent pool. We also knew there was no challenging, in-depth, and research-based mathematics curriculum to provide the services needed to nurture talent. Thus, a primary aim was to create, field test, and publish 12 advanced mathematics units that were both engaging and challenging for talented students in the upper elementary grades. In order to validate the effectiveness of the curriculum units, we undertook a research study to measure student achievement.

Identifying Mathematically Promising Students

Prior to identifying students, we needed to decide what mathematical talent truly is and how it is manifested (i.e., figure out what we were looking for). We believed that mathematical talent goes beyond knowing one's times tables and being able to compute quickly. In short, it is much more than doing hard arithmetic. We believed that being talented in mathematics is being capable of solving problems—real problems to which one does not know the answer or even the process to get to the answer. The ability and desire to think about challenging problems critically and creatively and to persist in solving these problems with high-level reasoning were what we were looking for (Gavin, 2011; Gavin & Adelson, 2008.) These, in fact, are the same characteristics that professional mathematicians possess.

In an effort to target underrepresented groups and support a more diverse and inclusive group of students, we also expanded our view of which students possessed this kind of talent or had the potential to do so. In 1999, an NCTM task force coined the term "mathematical promise" and defined it as "a function of ability, motivation, belief, and experience or opportunity" (Sheffield, Bennett, Berriozabal, DeArmond, & Wertheimer, p. 310). They also emphasized that students who possess mathematical promise have "a large range of abilities and a continuum of needs that should be met" (Sheffield et al., 1999, p. 310). We used this definition of mathematical promise in identifying students (both in the comparison and intervention groups) to participate in Project M³.

We found it necessary to use a variety of measures to view students through different lenses in order to get a true picture of their talent and/or talent potential. Because at-risk students often do not have the same rich experiences as some other students from higher SES communities, their talent potential can be hidden. We needed to discover this latent talent. Most helpful in this regard was the use of a nonverbal ability test. In our case, we used the Naglieri Nonverbal Ability Test (Naglieri, 1997), which was already in use in some of our field-test schools. This test includes items on pattern completion, reasoning by analogy, serial reasoning, and spatial visualization—all characteristics that would help our students solve problems and reason mathematically. In addition, this assessment helped us identify students from diverse cultural and language backgrounds and those with language learning differences because it uses only pictures and requires no reading.

We also used classroom grades and performance, any available standardized test scores, and other relevant information teachers wished to share about their students. Finally, we asked teachers to complete the research-based Scales for Rating the Behavioral Characteristics of Superior Students: Mathematics (Renzulli, Siegle, Reis, Gavin, & Sytsma Reed, 2009), which focus on such mathematical characteristics as using creative and unusual ways to solve problems, displaying a strong number sense, and frequently solving problems abstractly without the need for manipulatives. We combined the rating scale with other information that teachers were sharing into a Project M³ Student Profile provided in Appendix A, located on page 124. We used and recommend local norms for both the rating scale and the nonverbal ability test in order to be more inclusive in identifying mathematics potential when working with students from underserved populations.

Curriculum for Mathematically Promising Students

Encouraging students to think and act like practicing professionals is one of the hallmarks of gifted education, outlined in *The Multiple Menu Model: A Practical Guide for Developing Differentiated Curricula* (Renzulli, Leppien, & Hayes, 2000) and in the "Curriculum of Practice" part of the Parallel Curriculum Model (Tomlinson et al., 2009). These authors advocated for use of the skills and methodologies of the particular discipline a student is studying. We embraced this type of learning as the basic philosophy of our program. Thus, we created mathematical investigations that invited students to use the processes mathematicians use when they create and discover new knowledge. This focus led to a mathematics curriculum rich in reasoning and problem solving as promoted by the National Council of Teachers of Mathematics (2000, 2006). It is noteworthy to mention here that although the *Common Core State Standards* (CCSS; National Governors Association Center for Best Practices & Council of Chief State School Officers, 2010) were not written at this time, the CCSS Standards for Mathematical Practice mimic the practices of professional mathematicians, and students who work on Project M³ investigations employ these practices daily.

As recommended in the "Core Curriculum" of the Parallel Curriculum Model (Tomlinson et al., 2009), we built upon the key concepts and principles in each mathematics topic as outlined in the seminal work in mathematics education, NCTM's *Principles and Standards for School Mathematics* (2000), and used the research literature on how students come to understand these key concepts to inform our writing. Not incidentally, we also wanted the units to fully engage students and create a love and enthusiasm for mathematics. So, we included authentic investigations and interesting projects.

The authoring team was composed of university faculty in mathematics, mathematics education, and gifted education as well as a district mathematics coordinator specializing in gifted education. To allow for flexibility in implementation, the Project M³ units were designed as individual enrichment units rather than a single complete curriculum. The series is comprised of 12 units with four units at each of three levels, roughly approximating grades 3, 4, and 5. Each unit addresses important mathematical ideas from one of the NCTM content strands, as shown in Figure 2.1.

The content is accelerated one to two grade levels, and students investigate the mathematics in-depth over a 6-week period per unit. Students engage in mathematical problem solving, reasoning, and verbal and written communication. They create and use a variety of representations and make connections to real-life applications and among math topics (the NCTM process standards). The investigations demand high-level critical thinking and often involve the creation of

	Level 3	Level 4	Level 5
Number and Operators	Unraveling the Mystery of the MoLi Stone: Place Value and Numeration	Factors, Multiples and Leftovers: Linking Multiplication and Division	Treasures From the Attic: Exploring Fractions
Algebra	Awesome Algebra: Looking for Patterns and Generalizations	At the Mall With Algebra: Working With Variables and Equations	Record Makers and Breakers: Using Algebra to Analyze Change
Geometry and Measurement	What's the *Me* in *Measurement* All About?	Getting Into Shapes	Funkytown Fun House: Focusing on Proportional Reasoning and Similarity
Data Analysis and Probability	Digging for Data: The Search Within Research	Analyze This! Representing and Interpreting Data	What Are Your Chances?

Figure 2.1. Project M³ unit description.

products, such as games and culminating projects that encourage students to extend their learning. "Think Deeply" questions are the heart and soul of each lesson. These are open-ended questions based on the key mathematical concepts in each lesson that students write about in their student mathematician journals. With these questions, students are required to explain their thinking, justify a position they are taking, and even create some new mathematics. In effect, they are thinking and acting like mathematicians.

In addition, in order to fully engage students as practicing mathematicians and encourage the kind of discussion that promotes debating ideas and offering new ones, teachers are provided with strategies to set up a nurturing classroom environment. Students are expected to abide by the "Classroom Rights and Obligations" and teachers use specific talk moves to elicit high-level, participatory discussion. (*Note:* For more information on the Project M³ curriculum development and instructional techniques, see Gavin, Casa, Adelson, Carroll, & Sheffield, 2009.)

A Sample Investigation

To gain a better understanding of the curriculum materials, we present a math investigation from *What Are Your Chances?* (Gavin, Chapin, Dailey, & Sheffield, 2008), a probability unit in which students explore the difference between theoretical and experimental probability and experience the effects of the law of large numbers. This is a level 5 unit with concepts typically taught in seventh grade.

In the investigation, *Odd or Even*, students are given the game rules shown in Figure 2.2 to use with the spinners in Figure 2.3.

The question posed to students is: Is this a fair game?

Before playing, students are asked to make a prediction based on the spinners. At first glance, this game appears to be unfair. Students offer several reasons. They may say there are four numbers on one spinner and only three on the other, so there are fewer numbers to choose from on the second spinner. A more sophisticated response might be that there are four odd numbers and only three even numbers. When you add two odd numbers you always get an even number, so Player E has a better chance of winning. After playing 16 rounds, students may still think it is unfair based on who won their particular game. The reality is that although the game appears to be unfair, it is in fact a fair game. Using theoretical probability, there are the same number (six) of even sums that can occur as odd sums. The "Think Deeply" question in Figure 2.4 challenges students to be creative and change the rules of the game using their knowledge of probability and then explain their rationale.

Because our identification process is more inclusive, we know that the group may be of somewhat varying levels in terms of background and experience. Thus, in every lesson we provide "Hint Cards" and "Think Beyond Cards" to help teachers differentiate instruction. Figure 2.5 provides a sample of each type of card for this lesson

The culminating project for this unit is a "Carnival of Chance," where students create games that are unfair, but not so obviously unfair that no one will want to play them. Families, other teachers and classes, and friends are invited to the carnival. Students end the

Rules for Odd or Even

Number of Players: 2; Player E and Player O

Each player spins one of the spinners at the same time. The results are added to find the sum. If the sum is even, Player E gets a point. If the sum is odd, Player O gets a point. Play 16 rounds and record your results. The player with the most points at the end of the rounds wins the game.

Figure 2.2. Game rules. From *What Are Your Chances?* by M. Katherine Gavin, Suzanne H. Chapin, Judith Daley, and Linda Sheffield, 2008, Dubuque, IA: Kendall Hunt. Copyright 2008 by Kendall Hunt. Reprinted with permission.

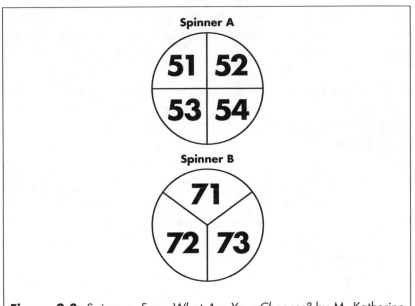

Figure 2.3. Spinners. From *What Are Your Chances?* by M. Katherine Gavin, Suzanne H. Chapin, Judith Daley, and Linda Sheffield, 2008, Dubuque, IA: Kendall Hunt. Copyright 2008 by Kendall Hunt. Reprinted with permission.

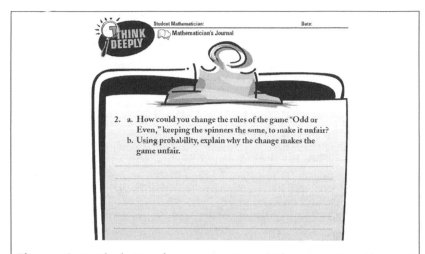

Figure 2.4. Think Deeply question. From *What Are Your Chances?* by M. Katherine Gavin, Suzanne H. Chapin, Judith Daley, and Linda Sheffield, 2008, Dubuque, IA: Kendall Hunt. Copyright 2008 by Kendall Hunt. Reprinted with permission.

Figure 2.5. Sample cards. From *What Are Your Chances?* by M. Katherine Gavin, Suzanne H. Chapin, Judith Daley, and Linda Sheffield, 2008, Dubuque, IA: Kendall Hunt. Copyright 2008 by Kendall Hunt. Reprinted with permission.

session with a presentation that details the theoretical probability of winning their game, and they use the proceeds from the carnival to donate to their favorite charity.

Research Results

We field tested the units with two cohorts of students, each progressing from grades 3–5 as they studied all of the units. We identified the comparison and field test groups in the same manner so that they were of like ability and similar demographics. The comparison group was selected and tested the year before the implementation of the program to help prevent diffusion of treatment. Ten schools from urban and suburban areas in Connecticut and Kentucky participated with a total of 20 classes each year (one intervention and one comparison class from each school). Although the majority of our schools had populations from low socioeconomic communities, we also included schools with populations from middle and higher socioeconomic strata. This was to ensure that we were not writing a compensatory curriculum for underserved students, but were indeed creating challenging and motivational mathematics for *all* talented students. Field-test teachers attended a professional development institute in the summer prior to teaching the units and three 1-day workshops during the school year. Professional development staff visited each classroom once a week to assess fidelity of implementation, judge the impact of individual lessons on student learning, and provide support to the teachers.

Our research questions centered on student achievement. We found that pre- and posttesting for all units across all grades with both cohorts showed significant gains (Gavin et al., 2007). We used the math concepts subtest of the Iowa Tests of Basic Skills (ITBS) to measure year-long growth as well as a more challenging open-response assessment using above-grade-level released items from the TIMSS and NAEP assessments. We found significant gains on both assessments from pre- to posttesting across both cohorts across all grades.

To investigate the differences between our Project M[3] cohorts and the comparison group, we conducted a series of two multilevel models using hierarchical linear modeling version 6.06 (Raudenbush, Bryk, Cheong, Congdon, & duToit, 2004). For all three grade levels, the results show our cohorts significantly outperformed ($p < .01$) the comparison group on the ITBS math concepts test with effect sizes ranging from 0.29 to 0.59. For the open-response test with the TIMSS and NAEP items, which more closely matched our curriculum and instruction, the results were even more impressive. Both cohorts' scores were statistically significantly higher than the comparison group ($p < .001$) at all three grade levels with effect sizes ranging from 0.69 to 0.97. Our research results for the project are reported in Gavin et al. (2009), which was bestowed the honor of Paper of the Year by *Gifted Child Quarterly*.

Helpful Implementation Strategies

To initiate Project M[3] curriculum and instruction especially in schools with diverse, at-risk populations, we share some recommendations based on our research. First, we reiterate that multiple measures of identification are essential to ensure that students with mathematical promise are found. Along with examining class performance and standardized test results, we highly recommend use of a nonverbal ability test as well as a teacher rating scale that looks at behavioral characteristics that are akin to mathematical problem solving. Even in our higher SES schools, we were able to identify students who had strong mathematical minds but were being overlooked as possessing mathematical promise because they were receiving special education services in language arts. Recognizing that many students may not have had rich prior experiences in mathematics, we also recommend use of local norms to be more inclusive.

Second, we found that most of the teachers in our study did not have a strong mathematics background. As elementary teachers, their area of interest and expertise was usually language arts. Thus, we offered more professional development than may be possible at the local level. This prompted the authors to incorporate more background on the mathematics being studied into the unit teacher guide. In addition, we included a glossary of terms for the teacher and specific teaching tips suggested by our field-test teachers who truly were our partners in research. For example, at the suggestion of our teachers, we included bullets on what teachers should look for in responses to the "Think Deeply" questions and possible difficulties that students might encounter. In short, our teacher guides provide an educative curriculum for teachers with detailed instructional strategies. This goes a long way with helping teachers successfully teach the units as they were intended. In addition, there are ongoing professional development offerings, such as workshops and webinars to assist teachers.

Implementation Models

Our curriculum units have been purchased by teachers and gifted coordinators in all 50 states and in other countries including Singapore, Hong Kong, and the Netherlands. The curriculum units lend themselves to a variety of implementation modes. If there already is an existing gifted program, the Project M^3 units offer teachers successfully proven, research-based mathematics materials for their students, either as enrichment units in a pull-out program or as part of the advanced math curriculum offered to gifted students. The Project M^3 units can also be used in a differentiated classroom to meet the needs of the top students. This works especially well with cluster grouping where a group of talented students comes together and the teacher has an opportunity to work with these students in a small-group setting.

If there is no gifted program, creativity needs to come into play! We have found that "Math Enrichment Clubs" are one way to provide this opportunity. As an example, for the past 5 years, Travelers Insurance Company has funded afterschool clubs in several diverse, high-poverty schools in Hartford, Connecticut. In fact, because many of our schools with underserved gifted students also provide remedial help outside of the regular school day (e.g., before or afterschool, Saturday, and summer programs), the logistics are already in place to service mathematically promising students. In addition, gifted summer and Saturday programs offered by universities such as Vanderbilt University use the curriculum with their talented elementary students and often offer financial aid to students who need it.

Contributions to Gifted Education

In conclusion, it has been very rewarding to create a mathematics curriculum to challenge and motivate young students to love math and engage in the work that mathematicians do. We have been honored to receive the National Association for Gifted Children's Curriculum Studies Award for outstanding curriculum for Project M^3 units and more recently, for our sequel series of the NSF-funded Project M^2 units for primary students for the past 9 years running. In order to maintain a competitive edge—let alone remain a leader—in this global and increasingly technological world, we must develop a new cadre of strong analytical and creative thinkers who can solve complex problems. These are our future mathematicians. It is our hope that Project M^3 begins this process.

As a secondary but significant positive effect of this project, we have found that our teachers have changed their teaching strategies not only in math class but in language arts, science, and social studies classes as well by using our discourse techniques to elicit higher-level thinking and discussion. For example, one of our teachers said that she will never go back to her old way of teaching. Teachers have also stated time and time again that their expectations of what students are capable of have increased greatly, especially for their at-risk students. This is so important because the first step in the whole process of developing mathematical promise is being offered the opportunity to do so. Our hope is that more of our young students are recognized with mathematical promise and that this promise is nurtured in ways that challenge and excite our students throughout our country.

Contact Information

To learn more about Project M³: Mentoring Mathematical Minds, visit http://www.projectm3.org. To find out about our latest NSF grant-funded project for students in grades K–2, Project M²: Mentoring Young Mathematicians, visit http://www.projectm2.org. All units are available from Kendall Hunt Publishing Company at http://www.kendallhunt.com.

The work reported herein was supported by the U. S. Department of Education, Jacob K., Javits Gifted and Talented Students Program under Award Number S206A020006. The opinions, conclusions, and recommendations expressed in this chapter are those of the author and do not necessarily reflect the position or policies of the U.S. Department of Education.

References

Gavin, M. K. (2011). *Identifying and nurturing math talent.* Waco, TX: Prufrock Press.

Gavin, M. K., & Adelson, J. L. (2008). Mathematics, elementary. In Callahan, C. & Plucker, J. (Eds.), *Critical issues and practices in gifted education: What the research says* (pp. 367–394). Waco, TX: Prufrock Press.

Gavin, M. K., Casa, T. M., Adelson, J. L., Carroll, S. R., & Sheffield, L. J. (2009). The impact of advanced curriculum on the achievement of mathematically promising elementary students. *Gifted Child Quarterly, 53,* 188–202.

Gavin, M. K., Casa, T. M., Adelson, J. L., Carroll, S. R., Sheffield, L. J., & Spinelli, A. M. (2007). Project M3: Mentoring mathematical minds: A research-based curriculum for talented elementary students. *Journal of Advanced Academics, 18,* 566–585.

Gavin, M. K., Chapin, S. H., Dailey, J., & Sheffield, L. J. (2008). *Project M3: What are your chances?* Dubuque, IA: Kendall Hunt.

Naglieri, J. (1997). *Naglieri Nonverbal Ability Test*. San Antonio, TX: Harcourt Brace.

National Assessment of Educational Progress. (2011). *The nation's report card: Mathematics 2007*. Retrieved from http://nationsre portcard.gov/math_2011/

National Council of Teachers of Mathematics. (1980). *An agenda for action: Recommendations for school mathematics for the 1980s*. Reston, VA: Author.

National Council of Teachers of Mathematics. (2000). *Principles and standards for school mathematics*. Reston, VA: Author.

National Council of Teachers of Mathematics. (2006). *Curriculum focal points for prekindergarten through grade 8 mathematics: A quest for coherence*. Reston, VA: Author.

National Governors Association Center for Best Practices, & Council of Chief State School Officers. (2010). *Common core state standards for mathematics*. Washington, DC: Authors. Retrieved from http://www.corestandards.org/assets/CCSSI_Math%20Standards.pdf

Raudenbush, S., Bryk, A., Cheong, Y. F., Congdon, R., & duToit, M. (2004). *HLM6: Hierarchical linear and non-linear modeling*. Linconwood, IL: Scientific Software International.

Renzulli, J. S., Leppien, J. H., & Hays, T. S. (2000). *The multiple menu model: A practical guide for developing differentiated curriculum*. Waco, TX: Prufrock Press.

Renzulli, J. S., Siegle, D., Reis, S. M., Gavin, M. K., & Sytsma Reed, R. E. (2009). An investigation of the reliability and factor structure of four new scales for rating the behavioral characteristics of superior students. *Journal of Advanced Academics, 21*, 84–108.

Sheffield, L. J., Bennett, J., Berriozabal, M., DeArmond, M., & Wertheimer, R. (1999). Report of the task force on the mathematically promising. In L. J. Sheffield (Ed.), *Developing mathematically promising students* (pp. 309–316). Reston, VA: National Council of Teachers of Mathematics.

Tomlinson, C. A., Kaplan, S. N., Renzulli, J. S., Purcell, J. H., Leppien, J. H., & Burns, D. E., (2009). *The parallel curriculum: A design to develop learner potential and challenge advanced learners* (2nd ed.). Thousand Oaks, CA: Corwin Press.

Trends in International Mathematics and Science Study. (2008). *TIMMS 2007 results*. Retrieved from http://nces.ed.gov/timss/results07_math07.asp

chapter 3

The Next Generation Venture Fund

Renée C. Haston

Introduction

The Next Generation Venture Fund (NGVF) was established in 2004 after a successful pilot program. Its founder, Stephanie Bell-Rose, was the president of the Goldman Sachs Foundation at that time. Her personal background and experience of being a high-potential student from an underserved population led her to target this population in order to strengthen its ability to compete and excel in rigorous academic settings and future endeavors beyond the classroom. Thus, the ultimate goal of the NGVF program is for these students to enter challenging careers and obtain key leadership roles in society. Although the Goldman Sachs Foundation remains the primary program funder, other donors including companies, foundations, and individuals have invested in the NGVF program.

The NGVF program, which begins in eighth grade and culminates with high school graduation, operates out of two locations: the Duke University Talent Identification (Duke TIP) and the Johns Hopkins University Center for Talented Youth (CTY). These two programs offer similar benefits; however, the specifics of this chapter discuss the NGVF program at Duke TIP, which includes students who participate in one of the following talent searches: Duke TIP, the Northwestern University Center for Talent Development (CTD), or the Center for Bright Kids (CBK). The NGVF program at Duke TIP presently serves 147 students (78 females and 69 males).

Identification of NGVF Students

To identify students who met the high-potential and underserved demographic on which NGVF was to be based, the Goldman Sachs Foundation partnered with the national talent search programs based on their national reach, their proven success of these programs in identifying and offering educationally challenging programming for academically gifted populations, and their emphasis on serving economically disadvantaged and underrepresented minority students. In addition, the talent search organizations offered an already established network of preexisting relationships with school principals, guidance counselors, and district superintendents to help facilitate the delivery of the NGVF program.

Talent search programs in the U.S. date back to the early 1970s when Julian Stanley, a psychologist at Johns Hopkins University, developed an above-level testing model to identify academically talented students so as to avoid the ceiling effects that on-level tests have for high-ability students (Stanley, 2005). Students qualify to participate in a talent search by scoring at or above the 95th percentile on a standardized test in fifth or sixth grade. Talent search participants then take an above-level standardized test (either the SAT or the ACT) in seventh grade; students who score high enough (generally ≥ 500 on any SAT subtest) qualify for participation in summer programs. These scores put all summer program attendees in roughly the top 1% of academic achievement for their age (Wai, Cacchio, Putallaz, & Makel, 2010).

The NGVF student population is currently 49% Hispanic/Latino, 46% African American, and 5% Native American. Although NGVF students presently reside in urban and rural communities throughout the U.S., urban centers have proven particularly well suited for delivering the program, as they offer a greater opportunity to develop a peer group among the local students, and their proximity to colleges, universities, and resources facilitates program delivery. However, rural locations have allowed for inclusion of underserved populations including Native American students residing on reservations.

Financial criteria used to identify NGVF students are based on the federal poverty level, which is revised each year. Household size and adjusted gross income are the two contributing factors taken into consideration to determine eligibility. These parameters allow for a family of three to be evaluated differently than a family of five ($18, 530 versus $26,170 in 2011–2012).

Students who meet the aforementioned criteria (i.e., talent search participation, family income) are invited to apply for the NGVF Program in the fall of their eighth-grade year. A comprehensive application process is used. Basic information (student name, gender, and school information) is gathered through an application. A student personal statement and a parent/guardian statement are required supplemental pieces. Both are asked why they want to receive the NGVF scholarship and what impact it will have on the student's or family's future. These statements are critical in gauging the presumed impact that this scholarship will have on the student and his or her family, the commitment of the student and parent or guardian, the understanding of the scholarship benefits, and the goals of the student. Parents or guardians can respond in Spanish or English, which indirectly gives the NGVF staff a sense of any potential language barriers the family may have to ensure optimal communication. A transcript and a teacher recommendation are also required.

Scholarships are offered to those students who best meet the NGVF criteria and depend on the allotment of spaces. A critical component is the contract that is sent when the student is offered the scholarship. This binding agreement, signed by the student and parent or guardian, ensures that program guidelines and requirements will be upheld. All students must agree to participate in all program offerings, maintain at least a B average in every course, and enroll in a high school curriculum that includes Honors, Advanced Placement (AP), and International Baccalaureate (IB) courses to best prepare them for college.

Goal of NGVF

"The goal," according to Bell-Rose, "is to enroll these talented, low-income youngsters in the most competitive colleges and universities and have them succeed there—and hopefully in that way develop into future leaders for our nation" (Mathews, 2009, para. 10). The Barron's Profiles of American Colleges is used as the NGVF index to assess college competitiveness. NGVF students are encouraged to apply and enroll at a college or university that receives a rank of 8 ("competitive") or higher ("most competitive" or "highly competitive) from Barron's.

Success Through NGVF Benefits and Components

There are three primary benefits to NGVF students: the assignment of an NGVF educational advisor, college preparation, and educational enrichment. During the program, the students receive these benefits delivered during a continuous 5-year intervention or pipeline of services aimed at having the students secure admission to a competitive college or university.

Educational Advisor

An educational advisor is assigned to each NGVF student with the responsibility of providing ongoing academic advising and college counseling throughout the duration of the program. Without such an advisor, students may not take the proper program of study that would allow them to be attractive candidates for selective colleges.

This could include students not being enrolled in the correct level of classes, not being enrolled in classes altogether, or being enrolled in the same course in consecutive school years; these situations have occurred and been corrected through the diligence and early intervention of the educational advisor. The educational advisor develops and implements an education plan to personally outline the student's projected curriculum. It also documents extracurricular activities, test scores, and leadership and community involvement. Recording this information visibly reinforces to a student the importance of an upward trend of grades and a holistic profile by the time that he or she applies to college.

The educational advisor also has the critical role of building a relationship with the student and family as well as with the school counselor. Consistent and respectful communication with the sole focus on obtaining student success eventually builds trust with families. Once this trust is forged, the educational advisor is able to ask questions of the student to gain insight as to the best college fit as well as offer personalized advice throughout the college application process. This trust also results in families feeling comfortable with the educational advisor advocating on behalf of the student. The educational advisor meets with the school counselor as needed and stays apprised of school curricula and local opportunities. The information, such as the timeline of upcoming college fairs, obtained during these meetings is shared with the NGVF students and families. It offers yet another opportunity for students to have access to college materials.

College Preparation

NGVF has been successful in achieving its goal in large part because it of its college preparation component. This includes simplifying the college application process into achievable segments by gradually building upon the previous step. Because only half of NGVF parents have a 4-year college degree, many are not familiar with the college process. A comment like that of one NGVF alumni is typical: "I feel like without NGVF, I would have been completely lost when applying to college." Consistency and repetition are reinforced over the 5-year NGVF timeline so students know what is needed to be a competitive college applicant. Workshops, held each spring and fall, are an optimal time to introduce, review, and reiterate pertinent college information. Sample workshops include résumé building and tips for a college interview, both essential as they are usually required parts of the college application process.

College admissions counselors and financial aid officers are invited to the workshops. They are able to offer detailed advice based on their expertise in their field. College admissions counselors often share information, such as fly-in programs, which provide students with the opportunity to visit campus at no expense to them. Typically, fly-in programs are not advertised publicly so the NGVF students would not be aware of them. Financial aid officers also assist to remedy the angst of affording college by simplifying terminology and explaining avenues to pay for it. The attendance of the college and financial aid representatives allows the students to garner additional insight and perspective as they reflect on college fit and applications. When possible, workshops are held on college campuses at selective colleges and universities to pique interest, familiarize students and parents with these environments, offer opportunities for campus tours, and emphasize proximity of selective colleges.

Essay consultants, who are current or former college admissions counselors, are paired with NGVF seniors as they apply to college. Through drafts and revisions, NGVF students edit and perfect their personal statement and supplemental essays of their college applications prior to submitting them. Thus, they receive feedback from those closest to offering college acceptances. Feedback is also given by college admissions counselors who review sample student portfolios, including a sample Common Application and essay, which approximate what is ultimately submitted during their senior year. NGVF requires students to submit this portfolio during their junior year to allow students ample time to familiarize themselves with the actual college application and allow for revisions before their final application is submitted.

NGVF students are provided with resource binders, including timelines to offer step-by-step instructions, to navigate the college preparation process. The resources are emphasized at the workshops but may be used independently as well. Other resources provided include webinars, private access to websites that offer college and scholarship information, and videos with specific topics to enhance the NGVF student's application. According to a mother of one NGVF alumnus, "NGVF resources provided us the necessary information and answered so many questions in making us feel good about being prepared for the decisions and choices made for college."

An additional resource provided through the NGVF program is test preparation. Through Kaplan, NGVF students receive SAT and ACT test preparation. This includes online, self-paced assistance as well as classroom instruction at testing centers closest to their residence or school. Kaplan also provides manuals to prepare for the AP and SAT subject tests. Given that high SAT, ACT, and AP scores are favorably considered by college admissions offices, access to this benefit enhances the NGVF students' college applications.

Enrichment

NGVF students are prepared for college courses through experiencing two residential 3-week summer enrichment programs at a university affiliated with their respective talent search programs. "The curriculum is fast-paced, rigorous, and innovative, and courses are similar to those offered to undergraduates in select, competitive universities. The courses combine elements of enrichment and acceleration and are not graded, thereby encouraging intellectual risk-taking" (Li, Alfeld, Kennedy, & Putallaz, 2009, p. 409). The summer program experiences allow NGVF students to interact academically and socially with an economically diverse peer group, encouraging their career ambitions and supporting their educational aspirations. In turn, their peers benefit from cultural exposure and awareness to newfound perspectives from a less privileged lifestyle. All students in the classroom are unified by an appreciation for the value of education.

NGVF students also attend BizCamp, a one-week entrepreneurship program. A key component of this experience is a presentation of a self-created business plan that enhances the public speaking skills of the NGVF students. This skill is transferrable to the college interviewing process, which is now required by some of Barron's ranked schools. The introduction to business courses allows for another educational experience that a student may not have encountered. This was the case for one recent NGVF alumnus whose interest in business was triggered through his BizCamp participation. He enhanced his public speaking skills through the BizCamp presentation at the local level and then competed at the national level. He became active in Future Business Leaders of America (FBLA), which he sought out at his school and joined as a result of BizCamp. As a current student at a top 10 university, he continues to travel nationally as a spokesperson for FBLA and is interested in starting his own business upon graduation.

Each NGVF student also takes an online course at a point in time that best meets his or her academic curriculum. This course is accredited and successful completion may benefit the student with future high school course placement that complements a transcript. Course offerings that NGVF students are taking, such as essay writing, include skills needed to complete college essays and prepare them for courses at selective colleges.

Challenges Addressed

The NGVF program regularly assesses how to best address the four largest challenges it has confronted, namely working with students remotely, technological access, cultural sensitivity, and financial concerns.

Remote Locations and Relationship Building

Because the NGVF students live in distant locations from the educational advisors, there are limitations on personal interactions. Educational advisors must rely on other modes of communication such as e-mail, social media, texting, and phone calls to stay engaged and interface with students. It is important that staff presence and availability are felt regardless of staff location. Thus, NGVF students are required to have formal phone conferences following each workshop where material that was covered is personally reviewed and reinforced with the student.

Technology

The digital divide is evident when working with NGVF families. Students generally do not have the same level of Internet access as their peers. Based on experience, NGVF educational advisors operate with the idea that students do not have a home computer. If they do, Internet connectivity is often unreliable or obsolete. It is common for parents not to have an e-mail address. Internet access is usually obtained at a parent's workplace, the local public library, school computer labs, or through a mobile phone. The primary reason for the online course benefit not being completed by the NGVF students is lack of computer access.

Due to unreliable Internet access, a heavy responsibility is placed upon NGVF staff to mail documents. Internally, a 3-week delay is incorporated to account for the delay of students without consistent technological access. This is critical as NGVF staff members plan to relay college deadlines to students, especially because colleges require online applications. Summer enrichment programs, which have also converted to online systems, have required NGVF staff to provide paper applications to accommodate the needs of the NGVF students.

Cultural Sensitivity

The NGVF staff considers needs associated with different demographics of students, which have disparate concerns and require different attention. The largest group, the Hispanic/Latino population, generally presents the following challenges: (a) the desire for the student to remain close to home, and (b) a language barrier. Educational advisors directly acknowledge and verbally recognize the discomfort at the possibility of attending a remote college. The Hispanic/Latino NGVF alumni travel to workshops and share their personal experiences of transition and success. This has proven to have the most profound impact because it is most relatable to the families. Having Hispanic/Latino educational advisors who are bilingual has provided comfort as well. When possible, workshops and college materials are translated into Spanish. NGVF parents become noticeably more engaged in their interactions and communication with educational advisors when this is the case.

Educational advisors have noticed an overall lack of motivation among African American males. Through conversations with these NGVF students and their parents, this has generally been attributed to the following: a peer group that does not share the same academic aspirations and is not enrolled in their advanced-level courses in high school, lack of a male/father figure in the home, and struggles with self-identity. Similar to the Hispanic/Latino community, NGVF alumni and staff from similar backgrounds share personal experiences with the NGVF students in hopes of creating a community that emphasizes academic achievement and engagement in spite of these challenges. Partnering with community organizations to offer support and encouragement when NGVF educational advisors cannot be physically present has been critical.

Financial Concern

NGVF families express the concern of not being able to afford their child's college education. The benefit of NGVF being a 5-year program is that it allows for discussions relating to this concern to be addressed early and often. Financial aid officers attending workshops are able to guide parents through completing the Free Application for Federal Student Aid (FAFSA) and the College Scholarship Service (CSS) Profile. By understanding and accurately completing these documents in a timely manner, NGVF students receive financial support to attend selective colleges and universities. Once students are admitted, NGVF educational advisors also provide fee waivers to cover college application fees, which relieves the financial burden. Possibilities of submitting multiple applications are unlimited.

Contribution in the Field
of Gifted Education

Few programs like NGVF exist, so it is uniquely meeting the needs of underserved high-potential youth. In addition, NGVF is important for the diversity of summer enrichment programs. It serves the aforementioned dual role of NGVF students and their peers both benefiting academically and socially through their interactions in the same classroom.

Findings

The majority of NGVF students are meeting the goal outlined by Stephanie Bell-Rose. The Duke TIP NGVF program outlined in this chapter has now seen 92 total alumni comprised of five cohorts who have graduated high school consecutively since 2008. Each NGVF student who graduated from high school matriculated to college.

Seventy-four students (80%) matriculated to a college or university rated as a Barron's level 8 or higher. Seventeen of the remaining students matriculated to a college that was not a Barron's level 8 or higher; however, the college that they chose to attend was the best fit for them. The other student moved to his native country with his family and enrolled at a prestigious university at that location.

All NGVF students who self-reported their standardized test scores improved their SAT or ACT scores after completing the Kaplan course. Also, all NGVF students who self-reported received financial aid and scholarships that met their financial needs. This includes full tuition scholarships such as the Coca Cola, Gates Millennium, and Horatio Alger scholarships.

Program Sustainability

The program has been financially sustained to this point through the generosity of individual and corporate donors, particularly the generous initial funding from the Goldman Sachs Foundation. The program award of $25,000 per student has made it difficult to secure ongoing donations. As a result, the NGVF Program as currently structured will conclude in 2014. Due to the impact that NGVF is having on high-potential, underserved youth, Duke TIP plans to continue with a similar but streamlined model incorporating the most powerful program elements (educational advisor, enrichment programs, and college preparatory resources). CTY has already transitioned from the NGVF Program to the Johns Hopkins CTY Scholars Program.

> "Without this experience, [my son] probably would have attended our local college without knowing that going to a major university was possible. He has had the opportunity to look beyond the horizon. In today's world, education is the key that unlocks our future and the programs made possible by NGVF has opened my son's eyes to what his future can be."— Anonymous NGVF Parent

Contact Information

Please contact Renée C. Haston (rhaston@tip.duke.edu) regarding the NGVF Program that represents students at Duke TIP, Northwestern CTD, and CBK. Please contact Rebecca Barron (RBarron@jhu.edu) for information regarding the Johns Hopkins CTY Scholars Program. Websites for the talent search organizations are as follows: Duke TIP (http://www.tip.duke.edu), JHU-CTY (http://www.cty.jhu.edu), Northwestern CTD (http://www.ctd.northwestern.edu), and CBK (http://www.centerforbrightkids.org).

References

Li, Y., Alfeld, C., Kennedy, R. P., & Putallaz, M. (2009). Effects of summer academic programs in middle school on high school test scores, course-taking and college major. *Journal of Advanced Academics, 20,* 404–436.

Mathews, J. (2009, Winter). Giving to the gifted. *Philanthropy,* 13–15.

Stanley, J. C. (2005). A quiet revolution: Finding boys and girls who reason exceptionally well intellectually and helping them get the supplemental educational opportunities they need. *High Ability Studies, 16,* 5–14.

Wai, J., Cacchio, M., Putallaz, M., & Makel, M. C. (2010). Sex differences in the right tail of cognitive abilities: A 30-year examination. *Intelligence, 38,* 412–423.

chapter 4

The Young Scholars Model

Carol Horn

Introduction

Can school be structured in such a way that all students are held to high expectations and have the opportunity to experience continuous intellectual growth? How can curriculum and instruction be used to find and nurture gifted potential in students from historically underrepresented populations? What interventions must be provided to strengthen basic skills and nurture gifted potential so that these students may be competitive with other gifted learners as they advance in grade level? These are just a few of the questions that guided the development of the Young Scholars model, a comprehensive approach to the issue of the underrepresentation of low-economic, minority learners in gifted programs. It is a model that embeds high expectations, powerful learning, and deep understandings into curriculum and instruction in order to find and nurture gifted potential in students who have historically been overlooked.

Young Scholars is a model, not a program, and supports the notion of providing equity of opportunity to all students so that any child who has an exceptional ability to think, reason, and problem solve will be able to participate in classes for gifted and talented students. It is a model because it builds on existing structures and practices and highlights the importance of bringing together four elements that must be present in any effort to find and nurture potential in young learners. The two-pronged primary goal of the Young Scholars model is (a) to identify giftedness in children from diverse cultural, ethnic, and linguistic backgrounds as early as possible; and (b) to nurture, guide, and support the development of their exceptional potential so that these students will be prepared for increasingly higher levels of challenge as they progress in grade levels. The model incorporates key components that are interdependent and integral to finding and nurturing gifted potential in diverse populations. These components include committed professionals, nontraditional identification methods, research-based interventions, and other essential elements that show promise for finding students who have historically been absent in gifted programs (Bernal, 2002; Borland, Schunur, & Wright, 2000; Castellano & Diaz, 2001; Elliott, 2003; Fullan, 2003; Van Tassel-Baska, Johnson, & Avery, 2002). Because the context in which students learn and the expectations of their teachers are critical determiners of whether or not gifted potential is nurtured and developed, Young Scholars are provided with powerful learning experiences that challenge and motivate them to move beyond existing molds and reach new heights. Implementation of the model leads to systemic change and a school environment that encourages continuous learning and advanced intellectual growth. Figure 4.1 shows the Young Scholars Program Model.

Committed Professionals

The Young Scholars model was initially piloted in Title I schools because they have large numbers of economically disadvantaged students and many students with limited English proficiency who may be at risk for failing state standardized tests. These schools also had very few students identified for gifted services. The principals were invited to participate by the gifted and talented programs office, and in the first year, 12 principals accepted the invitation, adopted the model,

| Leadership of principals and collaboration among teachers | Curriculum as the identifier of talent | Interventions, extensions, enrichment | Ongoing professional development for teachers and parent involvement |

Young Scholars Is a Schoolwide Commitment

Figure 4.1. Young Scholars Program Model.

and began incorporating the essential elements into their school community. Over time, additional schools were added as principals saw the value of the model and were willing to make a commitment to find and nurture gifted potential. There are now 80 elementary schools and three middle schools implementing the model, and each year that number grows.

The principals of the Young Scholars schools are committed to increasing the number of low socioeconomic, minority learners participating in gifted programs at their schools, and they play a key role in the success of the model. As instructional leaders, they meet several times a year to collaborate, share ideas, and tackle the challenges and concerns that must be addressed as they implement the model at their schools. These leaders are strong advocates for the students; they provide ongoing support to the teachers, and they ensure that year after year the Young Scholars are placed with teachers who know how to nurture and develop their gifted potential.

The gifted and talented resource teacher assigned to each school, other educational specialists, and the classroom teachers also play critical roles. Gifted services in each Young Scholars school are provided through a collaborative model in which the gifted and talented resource teacher works with collaborative teams of classroom teachers and other educational specialists to provide a continuum of gifted services that begins in kindergarten. The gifted and talented resource teacher meets with grade-level teams to design and implement differentiated lessons that challenge Young Scholars to learn at a faster rate, think on a higher level, and study advanced content through projects, research, and extensions of the general education program. The teachers and specialists understand that the success of the model is dependent on their combined efforts.

Find and Identify

An essential component of the model is the identification of low-socioeconomic, minority learners with gifted potential as early as possible in order to provide them with an educational setting that will nurture their potential and prepare them for challenging coursework in upper elementary school, middle school, high school, and beyond. Young Scholars are students who are not likely to be considered for gifted programs using current methods of identification and who, without that opportunity, are less likely to pursue advanced levels of learning on their own. Historically, these students have lacked access to gifted services, advocates for their high potential, and affirmation of their advanced abilities. Young Scholars are identified by principals, classroom teachers, and gifted and talented resource teachers through an examination of student portfolios, performance-based assessments, and nonverbal ability tests. Beginning in kindergarten, school professionals work together to find gifted potential in Young Scholars, and curriculum plays an important role as an identifier of talent. Model lessons designed to teach students to think on a higher level and multidimensional assessments are used to increase the prospects of identifying a broader range of gifted learners.

As lessons are taught, a tool called the Gifted Behavior Ratings Scale is used to help teachers identify and record behaviors that may indicate gifted potential in children (see Appendix B). The Gifted Behavior Rating Scale was created by Fairfax County Public Schools in collaboration with Dr. Beverly Shaklee, a professor at George Mason University. The scale has four categories: exceptional ability to learn, exceptional application of knowledge, exceptional creative/ productive thinking, and exceptional motivation to succeed. Each category includes a list of indicators that provides examples of what this behavior might look like in a classroom. For example, under *exceptional ability to learn*, one of the indicators states, "is acquiring language at a rapid pace." This would apply to a student whose primary language is not English and who is demonstrating an exceptional ability to learn a new language. In another category, *exceptional application of knowledge*, one of the indicators states, "communicates learned concepts through role playing and/or detailed artwork." This allows teachers to note gifted behaviors that may be demonstrated through alternative modes of expression, such as drama and the visual arts. The inclusion of these observable behaviors supports the notion that gifted potential may be demonstrated in ways that traditionally have not been considered. It also helps teachers find children who may lack the skills that are needed to perform well on traditional school tasks and yet have the capacity to think, reason, and problem solve on advanced levels.

Teachers at the Young Scholars schools receive extensive training in differentiation and culturally responsive teaching so that they will understand how important it is to take into consideration the diversity of background experiences that the Young Scholars bring to school. They learn instructional strategies designed to elicit high-level responses and ways to record evidence of gifted potential through observations, anecdotal records, and portfolios of student work. For example, the gifted and talented resource teacher may model a lesson on creating analogies while the classroom teacher observes and records student responses and behaviors. Next, the classroom teacher will conduct another lesson while the gifted and talented resource teacher creates anecdotal records of student responses. Ensuing conversations between the gifted and talented resource teacher and the classroom teacher help them find and identify gifted students who are at risk of not being identified through traditional methods.

As the Young Scholars model evolved, the Naglieri Nonverbal Ability Test (NNAT; Naglieri, 1997) was incorporated into the screening and identification process for all students throughout the district in order to help reduce cultural bias and to provide an additional opportunity for students to demonstrate cognitive strengths. The use of the NNAT helped increase the number of ethnic minorities and the number of students whose primary language is not English who received gifted services. It also highlighted the need to design curriculum and instruction that would strengthen basic skills while nurturing gifted potential. Teachers at these schools continuously review and consider multiple forms of data as they search for and build on student strengths to find and nurture gifted potential in Young Scholars.

Ongoing assessments by educators who have been trained to provide curriculum and instruction designed to elicit gifted behaviors may be the most powerful means of identifying gifted learners in low-economic, minority populations. As one teacher recently stated, "I have discovered that there are many methods one can utilize to identify giftedness other than merely relying on standardized test results. I am now a strong supporter of portfolio presentations and anecdotal records to illustrate a child's abilities and talents . . ."

Nurture, Guide, and Support

The Young Scholars model promotes the notion of continuous intellectual growth beginning in kindergarten. Multiage classrooms, looping, flexible grouping, and/or vertical teaming of teachers are examples of service delivery options that are used to support the students.

Young Scholars gain important skills and confidence as they create questions, search for answers, and share what they learn through products and presentations that they design. As their confidence increases, their motivation and willingness to take risks increases as well. For example, a group of first-grade Young Scholars recently created a slideshow presentation to teach kindergarten students all that they had learned about insects. As they designed and created their presentation, the first-grade students became experts on their topic and were excited to share their knowledge with their younger peers. Another group of Young Scholars in fifth and sixth grade explored the concept of a watershed as they learned their watershed address and discovered their connection to a nearby bay through their local streams. After an in-depth study of the watershed and problems that occur when it is not protected, the students decided to take action and share with other students ways that they could help improve the health of the watershed and save the bay. The Young Scholars worked together and designed a school television show on the importance of protecting the local watershed. This experience allowed them to make a real-world connection and to see themselves as problem solvers of an issue that impacted their lives and their community.

Although all children need learning experiences that prepare them to succeed in a complex and competitive world, students from low-socioeconomic backgrounds are less likely to engage in such experiences unless the school creates them. The Young Scholars receive specific interventions designed to develop and nurture their advanced potential. These may take the form of project investigations, problem-based learning, research, and independent study. The teachers in the Young Scholars schools learn how to create lessons that connect to the students' diverse cultural, ethnic, and linguistic backgrounds while they help the students gain proficiency in reading and mathematics. The learning experiences that they provide Young Scholars promote a climate in which advanced knowledge, understandings, and skills are developed, guided, and supported.

Other Essential Elements

It is important to emphasize that Young Scholars are held to the same high standards and performance expectations as other gifted students. The main difference is in the amount of scaffolding and support that is provided to promote and nurture their advanced academic ability. The long-range goal is to find low-socioeconomic, minority students with gifted potential at an early age, to raise their personal expectations, to encourage family involvement, and to prepare these students for the challenging and rigorous work of formal gifted programs. Learning experiences for the students in Young Scholars schools are coupled with professional development for the teachers and outreach to parents.

A summer school program for Young Scholars from each Young Scholar school provides the students with important learning opportunities that are extended and enriched. The summer school teachers work with the gifted and talented resource teachers to design an engaging curriculum that includes concept-based instruction, enrichment opportunities, field trips, and guest speakers. The summer school classes are multiage, and basic skills are strengthened through learning opportunities that challenge the students to think and apply knowledge on a higher, more complex level. For example, one class of young scholars studied the concept of conservation and what it means to conserve nature, culture, resources, and ideas. The students simulated the role of Earth scientists as they explored the effects of deforestation on soil erosion. Through experimentation and data collection, they learned how trees and plants hold the soil in place and "conserve" it for the future. A visit to a local wetlands park gave them an opportunity to explore the role of the wetlands in conserving the quality of the local watershed. Later in language arts, they read stories from many different cultures and discussed the power of the stories and oral language as a way to pass on traditions and beliefs from one generation to the next in order to "conserve" culture. The students also experienced the power of conserving their own ideas as they wrote and illustrated new knowledge, thoughts, and reflections in a journal or notebook. The ideas and problem-solving strategies that the students learn during summer school enhance their skills as learners and carry over into the school year. In the fall, each school site makes a concerted effort to provide Young Scholars with opportunities to grow and develop with intellectual peers from similar backgrounds. Multiage classrooms, looping, instructional grouping, and vertical teaming of teachers are all options that are used to support and nurture the young learners.

Professional development opportunities for teachers at Young Scholars schools include culturally responsive teaching, identifying gifted potential in diverse populations, and differentiating curriculum and instruction for advanced learners. Teachers work together and design lessons that connect new knowledge and understandings to students' personal backgrounds and life experiences. Poems, stories, and plays that contain dialect, relevant role models, and varying cultural lifestyles are integrated throughout the curriculum. Authors, artists, inventors, scientists, mathematicians, and other leaders from diverse backgrounds who have made significant contributions to society are infused into the entire learning experience. The teachers are finding that when students are given the opportunity to study a diverse group of leaders who have changed the world for the better, they realize that the traits and characteristics these people possess cross all lines of color, class, and culture, and their personal aspirations are enhanced.

A summer institute helps prepare classroom teachers to recognize and nurture gifted potential in low-socioeconomic, minority populations. National consultants with areas of expertise that support this work are invited to present to school teams during the institute. For example, the teachers may spend a day learning about group investigations. This inquiry-based instructional strategy actively involves students in their own learning as they formulate questions and collect information and data to answer their questions. The teachers may then implement a project investigation of the wetlands that includes photography, field experiences, and guest speakers. The students generate questions, research answers, and design presentations to share all that they learn with their peers, parents, and other family members. Parents are invited to chaperone the field trips, all of which are in local areas, and many then take younger siblings to the wetlands park or other sites and the Young Scholars become the local "experts."

In addition to the summer institute, the classroom teachers receive additional training and support through in-services provided by the gifted and talented programs office during the school year. For example, when Dr. Carol Ann Tomlinson from the University of Virginia was coming to provide an all-day in-service to the gifted and talented resource teachers on the Parallel Curriculum model, each Young Scholars school was invited to send two classroom teachers. This shared experience provided a common language and framework for the differentiated lessons that the teachers then created to challenge and engage Young Scholars during summer school and throughout the school year. On another occasion, Dr. Catherine Little from the Neag School of Education at the University of Connecticut was presenting an in-service on the models and strategies embedded in the College of William and Mary language arts units. Again, classroom teachers from the Young Scholars schools were invited to attend, and they were then able to use the models, lessons, and strategies from the William and Mary units in their work with the Young Scholars.

In addition to their work with students and teachers, each school actively works to strengthen the family connection. Letters, brochures, and flyers with information about the activities and opportunities offered to Young Scholars and their parents are translated into multiple languages and sent home in student backpacks. Workshops for the parents are provided by the counseling office and the Gifted and Talented resource teachers with a focus on what the school system has to offer and how parents/guardians can be advocates for their children. Parents are invited to participate in many of the learning activities. This active involvement provides the parents with ideas on how they can work with their Young Scholars at home. Parent liaisons at each school also communicate with the parents and provide additional information and support.

Challenges to Implementation

One of the most difficult issues to address in finding and serving high potential learners from low-income populations is changing teacher expectations of what students are capable of achieving. Teachers must experience firsthand the level of work that Young Scholars are capable of achieving and then share and discuss their observations and assessments. At its inception, Young Scholars started with dialogue, and the program continues to grow through powerful conversations. Conversations among administrators, teachers, and specialists ignite questions and generate discussions that lead to new ways of finding and nurturing gifted potential in low-socioeconomic, minority learners as well as new perspectives on the level of challenge that students from poverty need and are capable of reaching. As one teacher recently commented,

> I think there are a lot of kids who aren't really iden-tified because they are not as verbal as others. And sometimes the verbal ones that do like to talk a lot are not as gifted as some of the other ones who are the quiet thinkers and who come up with really out-standing answers.

Another teacher shared,

> I have a little girl in kindergarten who is quiet and yet is a very intense thinker. She made a comment one time when we were talking about letters and sounds. She asked if things had to be in order. She asked if things in mathematics had to be in order, as letters have to be in order to make a word.

A principal sums up the impact that implementation of the Young Scholars model has had on her school staff:

> Anytime that you do something to look at a child's behavior or performance in a different way, then you're going to extend your perception of what's going on. So the more we look at children the more we're going to find out about them. I think the more we work with Young Scholars the more potential we're going to see . . . Since I've worked with Young Scholars, my expectations have been broader; I have higher expec-tations for children who are able to perform better. Everyone has an idea of what giftedness is, but Young

Scholars has broadened my perspective about who is brought into that category.

Finding and nurturing Young Scholars in order to ensure their academic success is an enormous undertaking that requires the dedication and commitment of the entire professional learning community in each and every school. Schools can be powerful agents of change when they provide a context in which students are able to develop potential that might not be realized without the opportunities that a school setting can provide.

Contributions to Gifted Education

When giftedness in children is viewed as multifaceted and multidimensional potential that is ever-evolving in response to internal and external catalysts, educators take a more active role in searching for gifted potential among students of varying cultural, ethnic, socioeconomic, and linguistic backgrounds. The Young Scholars model builds capacity in schools to embrace a new way of thinking about giftedness in students that moves beyond the notion of giftedness as a static trait and supports the notion of giftedness as potential that can and should be developed in all populations.

The Young Scholars model offers new language and ideas for thinking about giftedness that embrace expanded beliefs about the nature of intelligence and the importance of nurturing intelligent behavior in children from diverse cultural, ethnic, and linguistic backgrounds as early as possible. These expanded beliefs move beyond an exclusionary vocabulary based on a child's proficiency in skills that are taught in school and focus on culturally responsive measures of a child's ability to think, reason, and problem solve that cross cultural, ethnic, and linguistic boundaries. Schools that make a concerted effort to value the differences that children bring to school and provide multiple opportunities for students to demonstrate their academic strengths ensure access to gifted services for all populations and embrace the democratic ideals that support social justice and equal opportunity for all.

The model also challenges educators to identify and develop services and opportunities that draw out and build on student strengths while encouraging students to be innovators and risk takers. A focus on student strengths leads to a deeper understanding of potential and a realization that many children have been overlooked, not because they lacked the capacity to think and reason on high levels, but because they were never given the opportunity to experience the challenge and reward that a highly challenging curriculum provides.

Research Findings

Once they are identified, every Young Scholar is given a special YS code in the district's student information system. This code allows the district to conduct longitudinal studies on the performance of Young Scholars over time in order to determine whether or not they are identified for gifted services, the level of service, and the courses that they take in middle and high school. Because Young Scholars may be identified as early as kindergarten, the code has provided important research data on the impact of the Young Scholars model over time. For example:

* Of the 5,266 Young Scholars currently in grades K–8, 50% receive Level II gifted services or differentiation in the classroom; 25% receive Level III services, which are direct services provided by the gifted and talented resource reacher; and 25% are in a gifted and talented center program, which is full-time placement with highly challenging curriculum and instruction all day, every day.

* Of the 4,432 Young Scholars currently enrolled in grades 7–12, there are 4,163 (94%) in advanced academic courses to include gifted and talented center, honors, Advanced Placement, or International Baccalaureate classes. Of the 94% in advanced academic courses, 78% are earning A's and B's.

Success and Sustainment Over Time

Young Scholars is an integral part of Advanced Academic Programs and Services for Fairfax County Public Schools (FCPS). Fairfax County Public Schools offer a continuum of gifted services, Levels I–IV, that provide all students with opportunities to engage in complex subject matter connected to the program of studies and helps prepare them for more challenging and rigorous classes as they advance in grade levels. Resources and units published for advanced learners, in combination with units and lessons developed by FCPS staff, support a differentiated curriculum framework in the four core subjects at every grade level.

Beginning in kindergarten, students who exhibit characteristics of emerging giftedness or who have specific academic strengths are considered for differentiated services or Level II services. These services are specifically planned to provide more challenging content, assignments, resources, and instructional groupings within the classroom. Level II services are provided in kindergarten through grade 6 by classroom teachers in collaboration with the gifted and talented resource teacher. Level III consists of direct services in grades 3–6 to students who have been identified by a local school screening committee. Level III services are provided by the gifted and talented resource teacher and include lessons that enrich and extend the program of studies in specific content areas. The gifted and talented resource teachers collaborate with classroom teachers to design differentiated lessons that challenge students to learn at a faster rate, think on a higher level, and study sophisticated and complex content in the four core subject areas.

Because it is part of the FCPS Advanced Academic continuum of services and not a separate program, the Young Scholars model is sustained over time through the ongoing work and support of all advanced academic programs in the district. With its focus on increasing the proportion of historically underrepresented students in FCPS gifted programs, the model has also become an important part of the work that the district is doing to close the achievement gap between White and Asian students and underrepresented minority populations. The teachers understand that the success of the model is dependent on their combined efforts. Teachers at the Young Scholars schools learn instructional strategies designed to elicit high-level responses and ways to record evidence of academic potential through observations, anecdotal records, and portfolios of student work. They also receive extensive training so that they will understand how important it is to take into consideration the diversity of background experiences that the Young Scholars bring to school. Every advanced academic resource teacher has been trained to implement the YS model and has been tasked to find and nurture Young Scholars in every FCPS elementary school.

Through flexible instructional groupings, a continuum of advanced academic programs and services, summer school, and afterschool programs, Young Scholars are provided an educational setting that raises their personal expectations, increases their self-efficacy, and prepares them for success in a global society with many complex issues and challenges. The Young Scholars model outlines essential elements and important characteristics that are supported by research and may be replicated in order to create systemic change and avenues of access to gifted programs that are open to all populations of students.

Contact Information

For additional information please contact:
Dr. Carol V. Horn
K–12 Coordinator, Advanced Academic Programs
Fairfax County Public Schools
Fairfax County, VA
carol.horn@fcps.edu

References

Bernal, E. M. (2002). Three ways to achieve a more equitable representation of culturally and linguistically different students in GT programs. *Roeper Review, 24,* 82–88.

Borland, J., Schunur, R., & Wright, L. (2000). Economically disadvantaged students in a school for the academically gifted: A postpositivist inquiry into individual and family adjustment. *Gifted Child Quarterly, 44,* 13–32.

Castellano, J. A., & Diaz, E. I. (2001). *Reaching new horizons: Gifted and talented education for culturally and linguistically diverse students.* Boston, MA: Allyn & Bacon.

Elliott, J. (2003). Dynamic assessment in educational settings: Realizing potential. *Educational review, 55*(1), 15–32.

Fullan, M. (2003). *The moral imperative of school leadership.* London, England: Sage Publications.

Naglieri, J. (1997). *Naglieri Nonverbal Ability Test.* San Antonio, TX: Harcourt Brace.

VanTassel-Baska, J., Johnson, D., & Avery, L. (2002). Using performance tasks in the identification of economically disadvantaged and minority gifted learners: Findings from Project Star. *Gifted Child Quarterly, 46,* 110–123.

chapter 5

The TEAK Fellowship

Katie Leh & Beth Onofry

Introduction

The TEAK Fellowship was founded in 1998 to help talented, high-achieving New York City students from low-income families gain admission to and succeed at top high schools and colleges. Named in memory of the founder's friend, Teak Dyer, TEAK provides academic support, leadership training, exposure to the arts and outdoors, mentoring, career experience, and assistance with the high school and college application processes. This comprehensive approach provides the rigorous educational foundation, robust academic and financial aid guidance, and transitional support necessary for academically talented, low-income students to be prepared to apply to 4-year colleges and to earn a degree in 5 years or less. After 15 years of service, it is evident that the TEAK model works:

* One hundred percent of fellows earned admission to one or more academically selective high schools, earning $35 million in financial aid for high school.
* One hundred percent of students who completed a 6-year fellowship graduated from high school and were accepted

at one or more colleges and universities, where they earned $26 million in financial aid.

* Eighty-seven percent of fellows matriculated to top tier national universities or liberal arts colleges, including 22% to Ivy League universities.

* Eighty-five percent of TEAK alumni are graduating from college in 5 years or less.

* TEAK's 100 college graduates include a Fulbright Scholar, a White House intern, an M.D., a pharmacist, five medical students, four engineers, four law students, four teachers, and a biochemistry Ph.D. candidate. Thirty percent have earned or are pursuing graduate degrees.

TEAK has identified six key elements in its formula for success, each of which is crucial in making TEAK New York City's leading college access and success program:

1. holding students to the highest expectations,
2. providing early and rigorous academic preparation,
3. using a holistic approach,
4. personalizing the student experience,
5. cultivating a positive self-concept, and
6. adding support during transition years.

Identifying the Correct Students

All TEAK fellows are high-achieving students who have been limited in their access to high-quality education and are living in low-income families and neighborhoods. TEAK is a selective program and applicants undergo a rigorous 6-month admission process. TEAK has strict admission criteria. Students must score in the 90th percentile on standardized tests, earn 90% or above in all classes, have one of the highest academic standings in school, attend a public or parochial school in New York City, be a New York City resident, come from families with financial need, and be citizens or permanent residents of the United States. To recruit students, TEAK shares these guidelines with more than 320 middle schools and community-based organizations across New York City.

However, TEAK not only looks at a student's classroom and testing performance but also at his or her potential through the presence of characteristics such as motivation, work ethic, resiliency, grit, and perseverance, as well as how a student has done in relation to his or her family, school, and community context. This is accomplished through individual, group, and family interviews, essays on the application, and recommendations from teachers and guidance counselors. Observing an applicant through diverse lenses helps decipher whether or not a student can commit to being a part of TEAK, and more importantly, if the student will thrive in and benefit from the opportunity.

Program Goals

In addition to a multitude of short-term goals related to each academic program and developmental milestone at TEAK, there are four overarching goals for the program. First, TEAK aims to help students build an academic foundation for successful lifelong learning. Second, TEAK strives to place every student in a competitive and enriching high school environment. A third goal is to ensure that fellows succeed academically in high school with ongoing, comprehensive support while they develop as well-rounded leaders and engaged citizens. Finally, TEAK strives to help students navigate the college application process and successfully transition to and graduate from the nation's most selective 4-year colleges.

The TEAK Model—In-Depth

Starting in sixth grade, TEAK's formula for college access and success contains four core elements that expose students to the full educational landscape and help them build a long-term foundation of knowledge, skills, experiences, and networks, enabling them to compete and succeed in high school and college at the highest levels.

Rigorous Academics

Rigorous academics must start immediately upon admission to accelerate learning, help close gaps in instruction, and prepare students for the highest level of advancement in the most selective high schools and colleges.

Middle school academy. This program for grades 6–8 is a cycle of experiential, hands-on learning to help build the foundation of academic skills utilized throughout TEAK, high school, and college, and to ensure that TEAK students enter their selective high schools fully prepared and academically competitive. Offered after school, on weekends, and as three full-day, 6-week summer institutes, courses include language, humanities, reading comprehension, analytical writing, foundations of algebra and geometry, science, Latin, and test preparation. Integrated into the curriculum are study skills lessons and exposure to the arts.

Research and writing courses. In ninth grade, a research and writing course about gentrification develops advanced skills in critical reading, note taking, research, and writing. In tenth grade, a New York City civics course challenges students to explore the city's complex governmental infrastructure and the intersection of public and private sectors.

SAT preparation. An innovative SAT preparation program is available to 11th- and 12th-grade students. It features individualized coursework, dynamic online materials, and a student-to-teacher ratio of 8:1 during instruction.

Specialized tutoring. From grades 8–12, specialized tutoring helps address individual challenges, subject proficiency, and the transition to college-level work. TEAK facilitates weekly tutoring, as needed, in a variety of subjects, as well as advanced coursework for those who outpace the class or want to enhance their learning.

Guidance

TEAK offers guidance to help students navigate their educational opportunities, gain admission to selective high schools and colleges, and secure the necessary financial aid.

High school placement services. In grades 6–8, these services are offered to assist in each student's search for the best high school match. TEAK guides each family through the admission and financial aid application processes at selective independent, parochial, and public high schools.

Individual guidance counseling. During grades 9–12, TEAK monitors the academic, financial, and personal status of each student. Via e-mail, phone, and in-person visits with TEAK deans, ninth graders have weekly check-ins and 10th through 12th graders have monthly check-ins. Students come together for workshops and forums at TEAK to ensure they are supported in their academic pursuits, have a strong peer network, and are successfully moving toward higher education.

The TEAK parents' association. During grades 9–12, TEAK facilitates an active parental role in students' educations and gives parents an opportunity to discuss the educational and social issues their children face, as well as their experience as parents of students attending academically rigorous schools.

College guidance counseling. In grades 11 and 12, TEAK offers individual counseling meetings, family workshops, and college trips in preparation to submit college applications, complete the College Scholarship Service Profile (CSS Profile) and the Free Application for Federal Student Aid (FAFSA), negotiate aid packages, and make final matriculation decisions.

Senior send-off. This program offers 12th graders educational sessions on academic expectations, time management, health and wellness, independent financial skills, and an orientation to the alumni program to facilitate a strong transition to college.

Alumni support services. These services for college students and recent graduates include academic guidance, financial aid counseling, school visits, and a fund to assist with educational expenses. An alumni coordinator meets with high school graduates to identify each student's specific needs, visits freshmen on campus, and performs e-mail and phone check-ins throughout the year. Quarterly e-news-letters, alumni e-mails, and LinkedIn and Facebook groups also help to keep everyone connected.

Professional Development

TEAK emphasizes professional development to highlight the complementary skills required for success in both the classroom and the workplace, and to pave the road for meaningful postgraduate career tracks.

Public service internships. This program allows 10th-grade students to give back to their communities and gain work experience by volunteering 150 hours at nonprofits.

Private enterprise internships. These internships create opportunities and real-world exposure to different careers and professional skills for junior and senior students. After résumé review, interview practice, and skills workshops, TEAK places students in paid internships at companies where they work an average of 7 weeks over the summer.

An alumni career center. The career center offers college students and recent graduates the resources and tools necessary to obtain meaningful jobs during college and to embark successfully on professional tracks after graduation. The center provides career counseling, résumé review, interview preparation, professional mentors, an internship and job bank, and an internship stipend fund to support alumni in unpaid internships.

Personal Development

TEAK provides diverse opportunities for students to develop as leaders and civic-minded individuals.

A mentor program. Throughout the fellowship, this program adds an adult advocate to the lives of students. With TEAK's oversight, students enjoy relationships with volunteer mentors by communicating consistently and participating in shared activities.

A community service requirement. This requirement encourages ninth- through 12th-grade students to complete 115 hours of service throughout high school at organizations that are meaningful to them in their local and school communities.

Summer enrichment experiences. These experiences for ninth-through 12th-grade students include a leadership development camping trip, as well as study abroad opportunities, outdoor education, and precollegiate academic programs through partner organizations.

Alumni fellowship initiatives. College students and recent graduates can participate in an annual reunion, workshops and panels, and opportunities to guide younger students through high school, college panels, and college visits.

Challenges

TEAK encounters challenges that impact the academically talented, low-income population, and the board and staff strive to identify and overcome these issues.

Academic Expectations

As TEAK students enter the nation's most elite high schools, many find themselves in an extremely challenging academic environment. To ensure that students enter high school on a level playing field with peers who have been in these elite schools since kindergarten, TEAK fellows undergo rigorous and demanding academic preparation. During high school, TEAK continues with summer academic programming, offers tutoring, and helps students utilize the support resources available at their schools.

Social and Emotional Support

Promptly addressing students' social and emotional issues is crucial to their ultimate success in middle school and high school. To monitor the status of each student, TEAK deans are in regular contact via e-mail, phone, and in-person visits. Frequent contact allows TEAK to address issues, to help students get timely support, and to outsource counseling when necessary. From the start, TEAK emphasizes the importance of being a part of a community of like-minded individuals. In class meetings, fellows discuss issues as a group and can often develop solutions to those problems together. For example, during a ninth-grade Fellows' Forum meeting, students discussed the challenges of making friends at their new schools. They learned that their peers felt the same and together they identified strategies to tackle the issue, such as joining activities to meet new people.

Awareness of Academic Options

A third of TEAK fellows are the first in their families on a college track; some are even the first in their families to complete high school. Because of this, working with students and their families requires a great deal of education about the opportunities that are available to them. Through meetings and workshops, TEAK works with every family to ensure that each is matched with the best possible high school and college option. TEAK also ensures that language is not a barrier to learning about opportunities and having ownership over this process.

Financial Hardship

All TEAK students come from low-income families, and although TEAK does not pay its students' high school or college tuition, considerable resources are needed to work with fellows and provide a meaningful experience that can vastly improve their educational trajectories. A fellowship costs $70,000 per student over 6 1/2 years, which includes individualized guidance, tutoring, test preparation, teachers' salaries, counseling, transportation costs, supplies, and more. However, TEAK believes that financial hardship should not impact the experience in any way; thus, a TEAK Fellowship is provided to students at no cost. "Extras" such as track shoes or music lessons may also be provided to ensure an equitable experience to their higher income peers. For example, one student received funding from TEAK to participate in 4 years of music lessons at his school.

Results

TEAK has improved—and continues to improve—the program to best serve its students in a changing educational landscape. A consistent focus on refining its programming has helped TEAK develop its extremely successful model. Paul, an eighth-grade TEAK fellow comments, "It is a great honor to be a part of the special group of people who comprise TEAK. TEAK fellows are innovative, think outside the box, can always adapt to new challenges, and create an ideal educational environment for themselves."

The following are the details about the six key elements in TEAK's college access and success formula.

Holding Students to the Highest Expectations

High-achieving students living in low-income families and neighborhoods often attend overcrowded and failing schools with little access to college preparatory academics, college counseling, summer internships, or exposure to the arts. Those who can persevere beyond the limitations of their schools and neighborhoods generally do not enroll at, and often do not even apply to, the most competitive colleges. This phenomenon, identified as "under-matching" by authors Bowen, Chingos, and McPherson (2009), plagues low-income students. TEAK's model, with its comprehensive approach to developing high-achieving students as well as well-rounded individuals, is a key combatant of under-matching.

From the time students enter the fellowship, TEAK holds them to the highest of standards—academically, personally, and professionally—and urges students to expect the same from themselves. Students are always at the top of their classes when they are admitted to TEAK; they are exceptionally bright, motivated, and driven to succeed. But the journey is only beginning and students are pushed to excel throughout the entire fellowship. TEAK has the highest expectations for its students, regarding the type of students they are, how hard they work, the high school and college they attend, and the type of citizen and professional they ultimately become.

Early and Rigorous Academic Preparation

When TEAK was founded, students were recruited in seventh grade and had one year to prepare for the competitive high schools to which they were applying. Over the years, the impact that early preparation has on future success became more and more apparent, and TEAK shifted and added to its model to provide more rigorous academic courses and test preparation prior to beginning ninth grade. Most notably, TEAK shifted the admission timeline to accept students in sixth grade, rather than seventh grade, providing TEAK with an additional 11 months to prepare students for challenging high school academics. Within these 11 months, a focus is put on language development and analytical writing—crucial academic building blocks without which students are too easily stunted in their intellectual development and educational trajectory.

A Holistic Approach

The primary focus of TEAK's model is on academics, but in addition to that intensive concentration, TEAK also offers enrichment programming to best cultivate personal skills, develop service-minded and professionally competent individuals, and create an awareness of and appreciation for the arts. All of these elements complement study in the classroom and help to ensure that students develop personal portfolios that are comparable to their higher-income peers, who often have greater access to these opportunities as well as the means to afford them. This approach also helps develop and energize students' passions, along with a lifelong love of learning, both in and out of the classroom.

Personalizing the Student Experience

An emphasis on personal attention and providing a close-knit community has become a hallmark of TEAK. Admitting classes of 30 provides each family a high level of attention and service, and academic classes of 15 provide each student with personalized and challenging educational preparation, all of which are necessary for placement and success in the most selective high schools and colleges. TEAK deans are in regular contact with all students to address any challenges that arise promptly. By setting up a support network, TEAK works with the student, his or her school and family, and other professionals to ensure that extenuating circumstances do not interfere with intellectual growth and success. Although this focus on personal attention requires considerable financial resources, TEAK recognizes the great value that a deep support system can offer a student on the path to college access and completion.

Cultivating a Positive Self-Concept

It is not uncommon for high-achieving students to be teased for being smart, enjoying learning, or getting good grades in school. TEAK has found that developing and maintaining a "positive self-concept" as it relates to academics helps students stay motivated and excited to learn throughout middle school, high school, and college. Being a part of the TEAK community and regularly surrounded by like-minded individuals who share the same ideals prevents students from feeling alone and further encourages them to achieve academic excellence. By sharing "kudos" with one another throughout the summer institute, for example, students honor each other publicly with words of praise and encouragement, thus fostering a culture of support for a job well done and taking pride in doing their best work. Emphasizing hard work—especially when it is challenging—and achieving one's highest intellectual and personal potential over "being smart" also helps students maintain their motivation and sense of control over their success when obstacles undoubtedly arise. Learning this primarily through robust classroom experiences at TEAK, and again through challenging outdoor leadership experiences, helps students to develop themselves and to transition to and persevere in new environments.

Added Support During Transition Years

TEAK's size allows for close, personal attention throughout a student's entire fellowship; however, providing additional support during the most challenging transition years is critical and TEAK maximizes its structure to best serve its students during transitional periods. The ninth-grade year, for example, can be a difficult year for fellows as they leave their familiar middle school environments to attend elite high schools. Almost half of TEAK students attend boarding schools and are also living away from their families for the first time in their lives. TEAK understands the challenges that unfamiliar environments, new peers, and increased academic rigor can present, and therefore increases its points of contact with students during this transitional year. TEAK deans are in direct contact with each ninth-grade student a minimum of 60 times during their freshman year through weekly check-ins, school visits, class meetings, and other TEAK activities. When you add contact with a student's family, TEAK mentor, and school advisors, TEAK has almost 80 points of contact in ninth grade. Similarly, during 11th grade, the most critical academic year and the start of the college process, TEAK has more than 50 points of contact with each student.

Additional Information

TEAK is 100% privately funded, by individual, foundation, and corporate donors and depends on these generous supporters to continue serving its deserving students. TEAK has received a 4-Star Charity Navigator rating—the site's highest ranking for fiscal management—which is a testament to TEAK's strong board leadership, sound financial health, commitment to transparency, and dedicated staff, all of which keep TEAK moving forward. TEAK also collaborates with many schools and organizations toward a common mission—making the high school and college experience as equitable and enriching as possible for every fellow.

Contact Information

For more information, please visit TEAK's website at http://www. teakfellowship.org; connect with TEAK on Facebook at http://www. facebook.com/TheTEAKFellowship; or contact TEAK's Executive Director, Lynn D. Sorensen, at lsorensen@teakfellowship.org or (212) 288-6678 x6.

References

Bowen, W. G., Chingos, M. M., & McPherson, M. S. (2009). *Crossing the finish line: Completing college at America's public universities.* Princeton, NJ: Princeton University Press.

chapter 6

Project *NEXUS*
Linking Middle Schools to College Success

Jeanne Paynter

Introduction

Economic disparities present significant challenges for school systems as they seek to prepare students for the rigors of college and highly skilled technical careers. Access to advanced-level courses is often limited for high-potential middle and high school students from low-income families. These students are less likely to maintain their high achievement, are more likely to drop out of high school, and less likely to finish college and graduate school than their more affluent peers (Wyner, Bridgeland, & DiIulio, 2006). Achievement gaps among low-income, high-potential students also impede their access to advanced coursework in high school. The report *Mind the (Other) Gap! The Growing Excellence Gap in K–12 Education* (Plucker, Burroughs, & Song, 2010) provided evidence that an achievement gap exists at the higher levels of academic performance. The analysis of states' test data shows that, whatever the effectiveness of No Child Left Behind (NCLB) was in shrinking the achievement gap at the level of minimum competence, there appears to be little comparable improvement at the advanced level.

Therefore, high-potential, low-income students are denied, in every sense of the word, equitable access to successful participation in advanced level coursework. Their means of approach to advanced coursework is impeded by documented achievement gaps. They are often denied the right to enter due to lack of preparation and prerequisite skills. The culture of poverty in their homes, neighborhoods, and schools challenges the ease of entry into a college-bound culture. The lack of advanced opportunities in their schools limits their increase in growth.

To address this pervasive need, the United States Department of Education's (USDOE) Advanced Placement Incentive Program (APIP) was established to increase the participation of low-income students in both Advanced Placement (AP) and Pre-Advanced Placement (Pre-AP) courses and exams. The College Board's Advanced Placement Program® provides opportunities for students to experience college-level courses while in high school, thereby fostering the critical thinking and persistence necessary for college success. The USDOE APIP makes 3-year competitive awards to eligible agencies to give more low-income students the opportunity to take Advanced Placement classes and participate in other challenging programs.

The Maryland State Department of Education (MSDE) has been awarded four Advanced Placement Incentive Program grants for projects spanning from 2003–2014. Through our APIP projects, we have been able to learn more about what works in providing appropriate programs and services for high-potential and high-ability learners from low-income families. We have identified and faced challenges and produced research findings that make important contributions to the field of talent development as a whole.

It is important to make the distinction between an AP or Pre-AP program and a gifted and talented education or talent development program. The College Board's AP program does not specifically target gifted and talented students, nor does the design completely align with the needs of gifted learners. The College Board states that enrollment in AP is for the student who is "prepared and motivated" and it "discourages the creation of 'honors track' prerequisites or other pipelines through which students must progress before they are allowed to enroll in AP" (College Board, 2013 para. 2). According to the College Board, a student's preparation for AP is Pre-AP, which does not consist of a series of prerequisite courses, but of the infusion of higher order thinking and learning strategies across the curriculum for all students. Although AP courses are described as college level and thereby offering gifted students accelerated content, an analysis of AP course curriculum has shown that differentiation within AP is needed to achieve the depth, complexity, and pacing necessary for gifted learners (Advanced Placement Task Force, 2004). Criticisms of AP have been that the courses cover too much and that the focus on the course exam results in too much "test prep." In addition, AP teachers typically have had no training in gifted education (Hertberg-Davis, Callahan, & Kyburg, 2006).

In Maryland, a state that until 2012 was without a mandate for gifted education identification or services, the AP program has and continues to be the major service provision in high schools that is available to meet the needs of gifted and talented learners. Currently, the College Board ranks Maryland first in the nation in the percentage of high school seniors who have successfully completed AP courses. Yet Maryland's urban and rural school systems, those with high percentages of low-income students, face significant challenges in developing successful AP programs, and disturbing discrepancies remain (Green, 2012). High schools that serve large populations of low-income students are more likely to have fewer AP courses available, thereby limiting access to advanced curriculum for gifted and talented students. In these low-income and typically lower performing high schools, the AP course and exam can become a benchmark for rigor and high expectations. AP curriculum alignment with the curriculum in feeder middle schools, which infuses higher-level thinking strategies and advanced content into their instructional program, can strengthen services for low-income, high-potential, and high-ability students in middle schools with limited gifted education programming.

This chapter will summarize findings and lessons learned from the evaluation study of Project NEXUS. This APIP grant project focused on the middle years as the *nexus* or "causal link" for access to and success in rigorous high school courses in preparation for college and beyond. The participants were nine low-income middle schools and their feeder high schools located in geographically representative areas across the state.

Our research study consisted of a time-series and a levels-of-participation design. The time-series approach allowed us to analyze whether there was growth during the 3-year implementation period and to a make a comparison of data before and after the start of Project NEXUS. In the levels-of-participation design, we categorized students and teachers into high- and low-participation groups based on the number of Project NEXUS activities in which they reportedly engaged. With the students, we were able to determine whether there was a relationship between participation and awareness of the role of advanced coursework in college readiness. With the teachers, we examined if their levels-of-participation in professional development and vertical team activities were correlated to their use of higher level teaching strategies in their classrooms.

The Goals of Project NEXUS

Between 2005 and 2008, the Maryland State Department of Education implemented Project NEXUS to expand opportunities for high-potential students from low-income families to gain access to challenging coursework that will prepare them for the rigors of higher education. The goals of this project were to increase participation and performance of traditionally underserved students and those from low-income families in Pre-AP and AP courses and exams; to increase student, parent, and family awareness of the college planning process; and to improve the coordination and articulation among middle schools and their feeder high schools to prepare students for AP courses and exams more adequately. Project NEXUS was also designed to increase awareness, beginning in the middle years, of all facets of the college planning process. Project NEXUS sought to meet these goals by implementing the following strategies:

1. Provide high-quality professional development for teachers and guidance counselors to prepare students for academic rigor.
2. Develop middle school English, mathematics, science, and social studies instruction that is vertically aligned with AP courses and exams.
3. Develop business and/or university partnerships and conduct student and parent/family outreach activities that promote awareness of academic rigor and college preparation.

Overall, these strategies benefitted high-potential students from underrepresented groups, as measured by their enrollment patterns in advanced courses and their achievement in those courses. The high school AP course enrollment and achievement data showed overall improvement. In more than half of the reporting NEXUS schools, a greater number of low-income students took AP courses during the NEXUS years than prior to project inception, increasing the numbers of students taking the AP exams and the percentage of students passing the exams (scoring 3 or above).

Project Strategies and Key Findings

Our research design allowed us to assess the impact of our key strategies of professional development, vertical alignment, and outreach.

Professional Development Opportunities

Project NEXUS offered teachers and school counselors an array of professional development opportunities, which included multi-day AP and Pre-AP summer institutes and conferences as well as school-based opportunities. Classroom walk-throughs and teacher surveys were used to assess the impact of the professional development on instructional practice. The degree of participation in Project NEXUS professional development differed across schools and in some cases, across grades. Our general finding was that teachers in schools and grades where there was a higher degree of project participation reported greater benefits for themselves and for students. Classroom walk-throughs using a rubric aligned with the content of the professional development sessions showed that the middle school teachers used a variety of teaching methods, including those designed to develop conceptual understanding. However, our general finding was that the higher order strategies (e.g., perspective taking, empathy, self-knowledge, etc.) and alternative assessments were used less frequently and by fewer teachers.

AP Vertical Teams and Instructional Alignment

NEXUS schools were charged with establishing content areas with vertical teams of teachers from grades 6–12 to design and implement instruction aligned with AP courses and exams. By year 3, all schools had increased the number of vertical team meetings held in each of the content areas, with teachers of English and mathematics meeting more frequently than their colleagues in science and social studies. A notable finding was that a school that reported a 100% increase in English vertical team meetings also posted an increase in English AP course offerings and student enrollment in these courses.

Business and/or University Partnerships and Outreach Activities

Over the project period, NEXUS schools formed partnerships with the Maryland Business Round Table and with postsecondary institutions to increase student and parent awareness of career and advanced educational opportunities. Schools offered career days, visits to area colleges, presentations by college speakers, and college planning events for students and their parents. Our survey results clearly showed that participating students and parents were positively impacted by outreach activities to promote their awareness of academic rigor and college preparation. Specifically, students who took advantage of five or more NEXUS outreach activities were significantly more aware of the connection between the quality of their school work and their college/career potential than were those who participated in one or no NEXUS activities. Similarly, parents who attended NEXUS outreach activities reported that they now recognized the value of advanced coursework, learned about college planning, and had conversations with their children about college. Despite these positive results, however, building parent participation in project activities was a challenge, and the majority of the surveyed parents in the targeted schools indicated that they did not participate in any NEXUS activity.

Lessons Learned From Project NEXUS

Our 3-year evaluation of the implementation and impact of Project NEXUS points to some noteworthy lessons from which all schools can benefit.

Professional development can make a difference. Teachers who had attended NEXUS professional development sessions were more likely to report engaging students in higher order teaching strategies—such as critical thinking, problem solving, and inquiry—than those who had not taken advantage of the training. These teachers were also more likely to recognize the importance of increased access to advanced courses for low-income students. In addition, teachers who were members of vertical teams were more likely to have fully integrated Pre-AP strategies into their teaching than nonmembers. These findings provide credible evidence to support the positive impact of professional development on teaching practice.

Content area vertical teams can make a difference. Although many factors can account for gains in AP student achievement, we identified a concurrent trend, which suggests that these results might, in part, be associated with the implementation of vertical teams. It was noted that when one middle school's English and mathematics teachers markedly increased the regularity of vertical team meetings with the feeder high school, the result was substantial gains in their

AP student enrollment in these subjects. These schools' students also posted growth in AP exam achievement.

Inclusive policies for student placement and academic support in advanced courses do matter. Greater participation in NEXUS activities increased student awareness of the connection between school experiences and future plans. The relationship held true for students from all ethnic groups. Still, in student surveys, most students reported that entry into advanced courses was by assignment. White students were most likely and Hispanic students were least likely to be assigned to an advanced course.

The majority of teachers reported that admittance to advanced courses was based on teacher recommendations and previous academic achievement. However, one middle school encouraged all motivated students to enroll in advanced courses and dedicated NEXUS funds to provide academic support for those who needed it. This school posted steady gains over 3 years in reading and mathematics achievement for all Pre-AP students in sixth and eighth grade. At the high school level, the school that instituted an inclusive admittance policy for entry into AP courses also made provisions for supplemental academic support; their results showed a sharp increase in AP student enrollment as well as gains in the proportion of students scoring 3 and above on AP exams during the NEXUS years. All schools can profit from these findings as they seek new approaches to increasing advanced course offerings, student enrollment, and achievement.

College and career outreach can make a difference for students and parents. This finding is particularly important to communicate among stakeholders who often question the relative value of participation in many or few such events. We found that our high-participating students (those who took part in five or more NEXUS outreach activities) were more aware of college and career choices than low-participating students (those who took part in one or no activities). Those parents who took part in NEXUS activities—albeit a small minority—experienced favorable outcomes. Parents reported that they learned new and valuable information about the importance of rigorous coursework in high school as preparation for college. They gained new insights into the college planning process for their children. It appears that Project

NEXUS outreach strategies have the potential to increase awareness of the importance of academic rigor, improve understanding of the college planning process, and encourage parents to become partners with schools in their endeavor to set higher standards of performance for all students.

Putting the Lessons Into Practice

Despite overall increases in AP participation and performance, at the close of Project NEXUS, low-income and minority students were not represented in proportion to their schoolwide enrollment. This disproportionality and persistent achievement gaps motivated us to pursue additional APIP grant opportunities through which we could implement and refine the lessons learned from Project NEXUS.

From 2008–2011, the Maryland State Department of Education launched Project 3+3: Access, Acceleration, and Affiliation = Achievement to expand participation in AP courses and exams within the Baltimore City School System. The three strategies employed to achieve these goals were *access* to rigorous instruction in Pre-AP and AP courses aligned with the Advanced Placement exam; *acceleration* of student achievement through Pre-AP and AP summer academic programs and seminar classes aligned with AP courses and exams; and developing peer *affiliation* through the establishment of learning communities such as Young Scholars.

Contributions from Project 3+3 have the potential to inform practitioners about the challenges of implementing AP programs in urban settings. Project 3+3 navigated the challenges and opportunities presented by working in an organizational system that is in flux and has been decentralized. With the introduction of school choice, a feeder pipeline of middle school to high school does not exist. Project 3+3 challenged school principals to become key stakeholders in the initiative and to take steps to impact the school's climate and culture positively to accept a rigorous curriculum and education designed to prepare students for success beyond high school. Students now have access to AP courses at schools where previously they did not. Project 3+3 contributed to a more strategic approach for expanding AP programs in the Baltimore City Schools. The challenge that remains is to build the pipeline of academic rigor that will increase the performance of those students who are participating in the AP program. One strategy being implemented by the city school system is the development of a middle years honors curriculum aligned with AP courses. This curriculum is available to those schools whose administrators and faculties choose to implement it.

In 2011, MSDE launched Operation ACCESS: Building the STEM Pipeline for College and Career to expand participation and performance of low-income students in AP courses and exams within four high schools and their feeder middle schools on Maryland's rural eastern shore. The value-added project strategies to expand ACCESS are acceleration, college and career readiness, community connections, enrichment, STEM courses, and student and family support. Middle and high schools will *accelerate* student achievement by implementing SpringBoard®, a research-based Pre-AP program for English language arts and mathematics. summer academies specifically targeting low-income students will jumpstart their success in higher level math and science courses. School administrators and counselors will collaborate to create a culture of *college and career readiness* for all students, particularly those from low-income families. Maryland's Chesapeake Bay watershed provides exceptional *community connections* to support *enrichment* programs that engage students in the STEM disciplines. A system of *student and family support* strategies undergirds the overall achievement of low-income students in the STEM AP courses.

Sustainability

We have had, for the most part, good AP and Pre-AP program sustainability in the school systems in which we have implemented APIP grants. This success can be correlated with a number of factors, including committed local school leadership, a systemic plan to increase AP, and ongoing support of AP expansion from the Maryland State Department of Education and State Superintendent of Schools. In schools that have not sustained their AP programs, the primary factor has been the change of administrator to one who does not have a vision for AP coupled with the lack of a school system strategic plan.

For the future, it appears that changes to the state accountability system will begin to focus attention on excellence gaps. In 2013, a new state accountability system, the School Progress Index (SPI) was developed to help educators gauge how well a school is progressing in its quest to improve performance for all students. In addition to achievement and growth, it focuses strongly on new measures of a school's ability to close gaps between its highest and lowest perform- ing student groups and for high schools to graduate students on time and college- and career-ready. The College- and Career-Readiness Indicator represents a combination of measures that include per- formance in AP or International Baccalaureate (IB), Career and Technology Education (CTE) Concentrators, or Enrollment in College. This emphasis on student achievement measures beyond proficiency may prove to increase access to talent development oppor- tunities for high-potential, low-income students.

Contact Information

For more information contact:
Jeanne Paynter, Ed.D.
Specialist for Gifted and Talented Education
Maryland State Department of Education
jpaynter@msde.state.md.us

References

Advanced Placement Task Force. (2004). *Analyses of Advanced Placement curriculum.* Abilene, TX: Region 14 Educational Service Center and the Texas Educational Agency.

College Board. (2013, January). *Required curriculum and resources.* Retrieved from http://professionals.collegeboard.com/k-12/assessment/ap/plan/curriculum

Green, A. (2012, February 13). Our view: Students top the nation in AP pass rates, but narrowing the gap between rich and poor remains a challenge. *The Baltimore Sun.* Retrieved from. http://articles.baltimoresun.com/2012-02-13/news/bs-ed-ap-test-scores-20120213_1_achievement-gap-low-income-peers-city-students

Hertberg-Davis, H., Callahan, C. M., & Kyburg, R. M. (2006). *Advanced Placement and International Baccalaureate programs: A "fit" for gifted learners?* Storrs: University of Connecticut, The National Research Center on the Gifted and Talented.

Plucker, J. A., Burroughs, N., & Song, R. (2010). *Mind the (other) gap! The growing excellence gap in K–12 education.* Bloomington: Indiana University, Center for Evaluation and Education Policy.

Wyner, J. S., Bridgeland, J. M. & DiIulio, Jr., D. J. (2006). *Achievement trap: How America is failing millions of high-achieving students from lower income families.* Lansdowne, VA: Jack Kent Cooke Foundation.

chapter 7

Project Athena

A Research Demonstration Project for Economically Disadvantaged Promising Learners[1]

Joyce VanTassel-Baska

Introduction

Finding concrete ways to help children of poverty develop advanced skills in the critical areas of reading comprehension and literary analysis, as well as persuasive writing, was the goal tackled by Project Athena, a Javits program grant funded by the U.S. Department of Education and developed through the Center for Gifted Education at the College of William and Mary. This 5-year project was implemented exclusively in Title I schools across a three-state region to elevate the literacy skills of gifted and promising learners, using a research-based curriculum as the primary tool of intervention.

1   Parts of this chapter are from "Project Athena: A Pathway to Advanced Literary Development for Children of Poverty" by J. VanTassel-Baska and T. Stambaugh, 2006, *Gifted Child Today, 39*, p. 58–63. 2006 by SAGE Publications. Reprinted with permission.

Identification

Project Athena employed the use of instruments sensitive to finding low-income and culturally diverse learners. It used both the Naglieri Nonverbal Assessment Test (NNAT) and the Cognitive Abilities Test (CogAT), finding more students than had been identified through the districts' traditional approaches. The majority of students identified for the project, however, were those that the districts involved in the study had already identified as gifted, those identified as promising due to strong reading ability, some typical learners, and some special education students.

Goals of the Project and Rationale

The goals of Project Athena were four-fold:

1. *To implement, refine, and extend research–based language arts curriculum units of study in grades 3–5.* The language arts units had been previously tested and found to be effective with high-ability learners (Feng, VanTassel-Baska, Quek, Bai, & O'Neill, 2004; VanTassel-Baska, Johnson, Hughes, & Boyce, 1996; VanTassel-Baska, Zuo, Avery, & Little, 2002), but work had not been done to expand the use of the existing curriculum with economically disadvantaged and nongifted populations of students. The special needs of economically disadvantaged and nongifted students, in particular, have led to the creation of supplementary materials to build thinking skills, such as the *Jacob's Ladder Reading Comprehension Program.*

2. *To develop and implement professional training models for teachers, administrators, and broader school communities.* Professional development training models are essential to the proper implementation of the curriculum and treatment fidelity. A positive correlate exists between teachers' use of higher level thinking skills and higher student achievement scores

(Sanders & Horn, 1998; Wenglinsky, 2000). Therefore, professional development modules are essential to the implementation of curriculum that emphasizes and assesses higher level thinking skills.

3. *To develop and implement instrumentation sensitive to low-socioeconomic learners for the purpose of identification and assessment of learning.*

4. *To conduct research on short-term and longitudinal student learning gains, as well as the mechanisms that promote the institutionalization of innovation through scaling up.*

The goals of Project Athena were initiated based on prior curriculum development research at the College of William and Mary Center for Gifted Education. The third goal, to develop instrumentation sensitive to disadvantaged students, was most critical. Students of disadvantaged means tend to lack the environmental exposure to advanced vocabulary, books, and the modeling of verbal skills needed for literacy and test taking (Barone, 2002; Duke, 2000; Grigg, Daane, Jin, & Campbell, 2003). Likewise, students of poverty also score well below the national average on typical standardized achievement tests (Grigg et al., 2003). Alternative assessments are needed to measure the full potential of these students and to determine what needs to be done to bring them to proficient levels of reading. Project Athena has employed multiple and varied assessment tools to establish baseline data on each student but also to demonstrate that different tests identify different students as gifted.

Finally, snapshot research agendas are not as effective in measuring the long-term achievement gains or nuances of curriculum for high-ability students (Arnold & Subotnik, 1993). Longitudinal research gains over time are essential to assess the long-term effects and implications of curriculum on student achievement. Both longitudinal and cross-sectional data were collected during Project Athena to document learning effects. Case study research on the most and least effective schools was also conducted.

Study design

Based on the growing research evidence about the efficacy of The College of William and Mary's language arts units with gifted learners, the team at William and Mary conducted a 3-year longitudinal study using the curriculum in Title 1 schools and inclusive classrooms with all learners (VanTassel-Baska, Bracken, Feng, & Brown, 2009).

Participants included a random sample of 2,113 students across 3 years and 39 experimental and 38 control teachers. Approximately 43% of the population was White, 27.5% African American, 18% Hispanic, 3.4% Asian American, and the approximately 8% additional students were of the Pacific Islander, American Indian, or Other ethnic origin. Gender distribution included 48% male, 50% female, and 2% not reported.

Using an experimental design, 39 experimental classrooms implemented a William and Mary language arts unit in grades 3, 4, or 5. Rigorous assessment was included in this study: an investigator-developed Test of Critical Thinking (TCT), the use of the reading comprehension section of the Iowa Test of Basic Skills (ITBS), and performance-based measures used in the earlier language arts studies.

The longitudinal sample for this 3-year study was 1,346 students, with 735 in the experimental group and 611 in the control group. Formal training for teachers in the implementation of the units was conducted for 4 days each year. Data analysis featured the use of multivariate use of analysis (MANOVA) to assess pretest and posttest results for differences between groups. Effect sizes were calculated for all groups. Results suggested that students in experimental classes showed significant and important educational gains in critical thinking across 3 years ($p < .05$) with effect sizes at the moderate level. Although students in the control group also showed significant gains in critical thinking, significant differences favored the experimental group with small effect sizes of $\acute{\eta}^2 = .037$. All groups within the experiment showed gains, including gifted learners, high readers, promising learners, and typical learners. Special education students also showed gains from the intervention. On the ITBS reading comprehension subtest, both the experimental and control students showed significant growth. Performance-based measures also yielded significant and educationally important results for the experimental students in all ability groups, suggesting that the curriculum is effective with a broad range of learners.

Data were also collected on teacher change as a result of both training and use of a differentiated curriculum. Pretest and posttest data using the Classroom Observation Scale-Revised (COS-R) suggest that teachers in the experimental group showed significant growth patterns in the use of key elements of differentiation (i.e., critical thinking, creative thinking, accommodation to individual differences) across 2 years of implementation of the William and Mary units of study in comparison to control group teachers not trained in the curriculum. Third-year results did not show added growth.

The results of this 5-year Javits project demonstrated the power of using more high-level materials with all learners, not just the gifted, as well as illustrated the importance of using multiple approaches to assess learning and multiple pathways for learning.

Curriculum Intervention

The program used the William and Mary language arts units at grades 3–5 and supplemented them with a new set of materials called *Jacob's Ladder*, a reading comprehension program intended to move students from lower order to higher order thinking skills in the language arts (VanTassel-Baska, Stambaugh, & French, 2004; see http://www.prufrock.com). Supporting the implementation of the program was a series of workshops provided to project teachers over the course of 4 days a year, 3 in the summer, and one at the end of the implementation period. These workshops featured the use of models designed to scaffold instruction in deliberate ways through the use of concept maps, questions, and core activities that engage learners in thinking about what they are reading and writing.

The intervention consisted of a minimum of 24 lessons implemented over a 3-month period at grades 3, 4, and 5. These lessons focused in an integrated way on the following curriculum goals:

1. developing literary analysis and interpretation skills,
2. developing persuasive writing skills,
3. developing linguistic competency,
4. developing listening and oral communication skills,
5. developing reasoning skills, and
6. developing a conceptual understanding (i.e., concept of change).

For example, each lesson to promote literary interpretation included the following components: (a) a multicultural literary selection, usually a poem or short story; (b) a literature web that required students to identify key words, feelings, ideas, images, and the structure of the literary piece read; (c) a set of questions to probe student understanding of the literature at a deeper level; and (d) a related writing assignment to encourage metacognitive reflection on the reading.

Teacher Training Model

The model employed to train teachers built on the curriculum itself by providing teachers the models for teaching the unit and then providing them the material to implement in the process. Each workshop segment was organized according to the structure of (a) introducing the model for teaching, (b) providing practice using the model, and (c) debriefing the model with the teachers. Collaborative learning was stressed as teachers worked in small groups to learn the models. For example, in order to use the literature web just described, teachers would read a poem, complete a web individually, discuss it with their group, and participate in a whole-group discussion of the poem with the workshop facilitator. Based on this process, teachers would then reflect on what they had done, analyze the processes employed in the lesson, and raise questions and concerns about implementing the strategy with their learners. For many training sessions, this format would be augmented by a video, showing how the web was used in a comparable classroom setting with comparable learners.

The multiday workshops each featured instruction in at least two such models each day, providing both the structure and practice for teaching. A sample workshop day schedule that featured the literature web would be:

1. Introduction of the literature web and its components (30 minutes);
2. Whole-group, researcher-modeled lesson using a poem or short story from one of the units (45 minutes);
3. Debriefing of the lesson, modeled with discussion of the observed teacher stance, research on teacher stance, and a discussion of implementation strategies—including a question and answer period (45 minutes); and
4. Reading of a longer passage and small-group practice in grade levels using the literature web, with researcher feedback (60 minutes).

The workshop model employed for writing connected the areas of reading and writing via the prompt provided. The use of the writing hamburger model integrates reading and writing skills by requiring students to think about the literature they are reading and decide if it should be required for students their age. Teachers were led through a power writing exercise that gave them 10 minutes to respond to the prompt, using a persuasive writing model that requires a claim, supporting data, and a warrant. They then read their selections and assessed whether the structure had been followed, using a carefully designed rubric. Such an exercise was encouraged for use with students to give them practice writing to a prompt in order to build fluency of response.

Results from data collected on the implementation of the curriculum in Athena classrooms suggested that teachers showed both statistically significant and educationally important growth patterns in the use of the differentiation skills of critical thinking, creative thinking, and accommodation to individual differences after 2 years of such training coupled with the use of the curriculum already differentiated in design.

Teachers appeared to enjoy the nature of the training experience and believed that it benefits students to a great extent. Feedback from the training sessions included comments such as:

* "I very much enjoy the hands-on activities that had us actually using the materials and working together through common problems that we had."
* "I'm so excited to get started . . . the workshop made me analyze my teaching. I am more aware of what I've done and where I am going."

Assessment of Students

Project Athena students were assessed on a pre- and postdesign that tested the extent of growth gains in the dimensions of critical thinking, general reading comprehension, specific curriculum-based proficiency in literary analysis and persuasive writing, and state proficiency in language arts. Specific instruments, either designed for the project or found through research, were employed. A brief description of each assessment tool follows.

Test of Critical Thinking (TCT)

The TCT was designed by the Center for Gifted Education for Project Athena (Bracken, Bai, Fithian, Lamprecht, Little, & Quek, 2003). The test uses Paul's Reasoning Model (1992) as a conceptual framework for the assessment. There are 10 scenarios and 45 questions based on those scenarios. Internal consistency coefficients are high: grade 3 is .85, grade 4 is .83, and grade 5 is .87. The total sample is .89. Experts knowledgeable about Paul's Reasoning Model and critical thinking elements also assessed content validity. Construct validity is yet to be determined. Based on the pilot data and data from Project Athena, the test has a strong floor and ceiling (-2 standard deviations to +2 standard deviations), therefore exhibiting sufficient range for the exceptional students assessed with this measure.

Iowa Test of Basic Skills (ITBS)

The ITBS is a longstanding standardized assessment that has been in existence since 1935 and has regular renorming procedures. The reading comprehension section of this assessment was used to determine the pre- and postcomprehension levels of students. Reliability coefficients are higher for the subtest of reading comprehension at each grade level. Grade 3 reading ranged from .88 to .89, grade 4 from .87 to 88, and grade 5 ranged from .86 to .87. Standard error of measurement was between 2.1 and 2.5.

Performance-Based Assessments

Pre- and postperformance-based reading and writing assessments were also administered to the experimental group only. Modeling after the National Assessment of Educational Progress (NAEP) in reading, content validity and reliability of both measures has been assessed and found to be appropriate. The literary analysis assessment consists of four questions about a particular reading. Questions require inference, interpretation, and conceptual thinking. Similarly, the persuasive writing assessment provides a prompt that students must respond to based on a particular reading (e.g., Should this story be required reading for your grade level?) Rubrics were designed to measure the appropriateness of responses for each assessment. The rubric was based on Toulmin's (1958) criteria for judging the quality of claim, data, and warrant, as adapted by Burkhalter (1995). Interrater reliability on the writing rubric has been reported as .77 for claim, .56 for data, and .66 for warrant (Connor, 1990).

Assessment of Teachers

Just as students were assessed in the project for indicators of learning, so too were their teachers. The teachers were observed twice each year during the implementation period to ensure fidelity of implementation of the curriculum but also to assess the degree of effectiveness in using differentiation strategies that promote higher level thinking and problem solving. The instrument employed to conduct these assessments was the Classroom Observation Scale—Revised, COS-R (VanTassel-Baska, Avery, Drummond, Struck, Feng, & Stambaugh, 2004). The form measures differences in instructional behavior and includes six subscales: curriculum planning and delivery, accommodations for individual differences, problem solving, critical thinking, creative thinking, and research.

The overall interrater reliability of the COS-R is very high at .91 and .93, based on two separate observations. Subscale data were also collated, ranging from .67 to .94. Content validity of .98 was determined by expert review of the form prior to Project Athena implementation.

Findings

Findings on both student learning and teacher learning appeared promising and may be summarized in the following way:

1. Experimental students did significantly better than control students in both critical thinking and comprehension.
2. Gender effects were minimal.
3. All ability groups and ethnic groups registered significant growth gains from using the curriculum.
4. Experimental teachers scored significantly higher on both the frequency of use and effective use of differentiated strategies across 2 years. Growth gains for teacher use of differentiation strategies remained stagnant in the third year.

5. Experimental teachers who had used the curriculum for 2 years and received commensurate training demonstrated significantly enhanced use of differentiated strategies over first-year experimental teachers.

Barriers to Providing Appropriate Programs and Services for High Potential/Ability Learners from Low-Income Populations

Teacher Preparation

Most of the teachers in the program needed stronger backgrounds in working with gifted learners as well as using more complex materials. The teachers asked for supplementary materials, for example, that provided additional scaffolding for moving students from basic reading comprehension to critical reading. The project staff responded by creating Jacob's Ladder materials that addressed the request. These new materials provided the additional support needed and reassured the teachers that their students could successfully reach higher levels of thinking.

Flexibility in Classroom and School Organization

Neither the schools nor the classrooms involved in the project had sufficient flexibility in implementing innovation. Most employed rigid pacing guides, management techniques, and prescriptive approaches to curriculum and assessment that hampered faithful implementation of a new project.

Lack of Valuing Research in Practical Settings

Collecting research data in practice settings that lack adequate control systems to carry out such procedures is a major obstacle. Even with weekly assistance to support teachers, the data issues were challenging, from administering assessments to collecting them and scoring the results for use in instruction.

Fidelity of Implementation

A major problem for Project Athena was fidelity of implementation. Often, schedules of implementation could not be maintained due to circumstances including teacher illness, other curricula that took precedence, or principal intervention to ensure a building initiative was given priority. Teacher autonomy with respect to how and when implementation occurred also was a distracting condition that led to irregular and interrupted intervention time. Often lessons were not completely taught due to time restrictions.

Principal Support for Teacher Experimentation

Although all principals in the project pledged support to the implementation process, they had difficulty keeping it as a centerpiece for the school's work across 3 years. Competing curriculum and instructional approaches to reading and language arts were difficult to tackle, as entire staffs had been socialized to these approaches. For example, principals often failed to see the importance of focusing on promising learners who were disadvantaged, preferring to see all students in the same way. Finally, many of these schools had multiple innovative projects in place, splitting the attention of both administrators and teachers to implement them successfully.

Important Contributions to Gifted Education

Historically, the Center for Gifted Education at the College of William and Mary has been known for its strong curriculum contribution to the field. However, the contributions of Project Athena extended beyond just its curriculum to the construction of professional development modules that prepared educators to implement the program effectively to research studies that demonstrated efficacy in student and teacher learning.

For low-income promising learners, Project Athena has provided the *Jacob's Ladder Reading Comprehension Program* that scaffolds reading comprehension skills. These materials incorporate differentiation techniques for the gifted and are tailored for use with this special population of gifted learners. The Jacob's Ladder materials have been expanded for use in grades K–9 (see http://www.prufrock.com).

The research-based nature of the program provides credibility for replication and continued use of the materials. Findings have shown learning gains in reading comprehension and literary analysis, persuasive writing, and critical thinking.

Professional development modules have been developed that provide both teachers and administrators the training necessary to implement Project Athena components effectively. Administrator training focuses on the ways the program interfaces with standards and the management models of building and district implementation for literacy.

Conclusion

Developing the literacy of children from impoverished backgrounds can be done through a systematic approach that involves high-powered curriculum wedded to the use of powerful teaching and learning models linked to multiple modes of student assessment in order to gauge the level and extent of learning accrued. This approach can only be successful, however, if it is also integrated with a concomitant model for teacher training that stresses the importance of faithful implementation of units of study. Together, such components can spell the difference between high levels of student challenge and excitement in learning versus disengaged, apathetic learners subjected to low-level skill sheets.

Program Sustenance

The curriculum components of Project Athena have been sustained for the past 7 years and have been expanded to new districts during that time. Jacob's Ladder has been added as a means for scaffolding reading comprehension for use in many classrooms nationwide. Two dissertations have been conducted on its efficacy, showing significant growth for students in reading comprehension and critical thinking. Costs for implementation include a fee for professional development services through the Center for Gifted Education or the authors of the materials, and fees for materials, procured directly from the publishing company.

School districts sustain the use of the curriculum from Project Athena by allocating funds to purchase materials and provide professional development to teachers. Usually this funding comes from ongoing operational budgets within the school district and/or the school, from Title I funds, or from gifted education budget sources.

Contact Information

Contact regarding Project Athena should be addressed to Center for Gifted Education, PO Box 8795, College of William and Mary, Williamsburg, VA 23187.

The work reported herein was supported by the U. S. Department of Education, Jacob K., Javits Gifted and Talented Students Program under Award Number S206A0040095. The opinions, conclusions, and recommendations expressed in this chapter are those of the author and do not necessarily reflect the position or policies of the U.S. Department of Education.

References

Arnold, K., & Subotnik, R. (1993). *Beyond Terman*. Norwood, NJ: Ablex.

Barone, D. (2002). Literacy teaching and learning in two kindergarten classrooms in a school labeled at-risk. *Elementary School Journal, 102*, 415–443.

Bracken, B., Bai, W., Fithian, E., Lamprecht, S., Little, C., & Quek, C. (2003). *The Test of Critical Thinking*. Williamsburg, VA: Center for Gifted Education.

Burkhalter, N. (1995). A Vygotsky-based curriculum for teaching persuasive writing in the elementary grades. *Language Arts, 72*, 192–196.

Connor, U. (1990). Linguistic/rhetorical measures for international student writing. *Research in the Teaching of English, 24*, 67–87.

Duke, N. (2000). For the rich it's richer: Print experiences and environments offered to children in very low and very high-socioeconomic status first-grade classrooms. *American Educational Research Journal, 37*, 441–478.

Feng, A. X., VanTassel-Baska, J., Quek, C., Bai, W., & O'Neill, B. (2004). A longitudinal assessment of gifted students' learning using the Integrated Curriculum Model: Impacts and perceptions of the William and Mary language arts and science curriculum. *Roeper Review, 27*, 78–83.

Grigg, W. S., Daane, M. C., Jin, Y., & Campbell, J. R. (2003). *The nation's report card: Reading 2002*. Washington, DC: National Center for Education Statistics.

Paul, R. (1992). *Critical thinking: What every person needs to survive in a rapidly changing world*. Sonoma, CA: The Foundation for Critical Thinking.

Sanders, W. L., & Horn, S. P. (1998). Research findings from the Tennessee value-added assessment system (TVAAS) database: Implications for educational evaluation and research. *Journal of Personnel Evaluation in Education, 12*, 247–256.

Toulmin, S. E. (1958). *The uses of argument.* Cambridge, England: Cambridge University Press.

VanTassel-Baska, J., Avery, L., Drummond, D., Struck, J., Feng, A. X., & Stambaugh, T. (2004). *Classroom observation scale-revised.* Williamsburg, VA: Center for Gifted Education.

VanTassel-Baska, J., Bracken, B., Feng, A., & Brown E. (2009). A longitudinal study of reading comprehension and reasoning ability of students in elementary Title I schools, *Journal for the Education of the Gifted, 33,* 7–37.

VanTassel-Baska, J., Johnson, D., Hughes, C., & Boyce, L. N. (1996). A study of the language arts curriculum effectives with gifted learners. *Journal for the Education of the Gifted, 19,* 461–468.

VanTassel-Baska, J., & Stambaugh, T. (2006). Project Athena: A pathway to advanced literary development for children of poverty. *Gifted Child Today, 39,* 58–63.

VanTassel-Baska, J., Stambaugh, T., & French, H. (2004). *Jacob's ladder reading comprehension program.* Williamsburg, VA: Center for Gifted Education.

VanTassel-Baska, J., Zuo, L., Avery, L. D., & Little, C. A. (2002). A curriculum study of gifted student learning in the language arts. *Gifted Child Quarterly, 46,* 30–44.

Wenglinsky, H. (2000). *How teaching matters: Bringing the classroom back into discussions of teacher quality.* Princeton, NJ: The Milken Family Foundation and Educational Testing Service.

chapter 8

Project Clarion

Joyce VanTassel-Baska

Introduction

Project Clarion, a 5-year scale-up Javits project, was one response to a set of interconnected problems that have thwarted the development of scientific talent in young children (National Science Board, 2010), failed to develop scientific talent at early childhood levels of the curriculum, and ignored the importance of developing talent in promising students from poverty (VanTassel-Baska, 2010). The purpose of the project was to target low-income, high-ability learners and measure the effects of higher level, inquiry-based science curricula on their learning. Specific project objectives included: (a) implement instrumentation sensitive to low-socioeconomic learners for purposes of enhanced identification and assessment of learning; (b) write, implement, refine, and extend research-based concept curriculum units of study from Pre-K through third grade; (c) develop and implement professional training models for teachers, administrators, and broader school communities; and (d) conduct research on short-term and longitudinal student learning gains, as well as investigate the mechanisms that promote institutionalization of innovation through curriculum scaling up.

How Are Students Identified for the Program? What Talents Are Valued?

Selection for Project Clarion used existing identification protocols employed by the schools to identify participants. Project staff encouraged the use of nonverbal measures along with other approaches employed by districts. They also encouraged the identification of promising learners, students who had not yet been formally identified as gifted but who were on the cusp of being so based on test data, performance in class, and recommendations from relevant personnel in the district. There also was an attempt to find students who showed interest and curiosity about science and who demonstrated scientific skills of observation and questioning. In this project, we clearly valued an inquiring mind as a centerpiece of potential talent in science as much as or more than other concrete measures of ability.

The sample of traditionally underserved students was comprised of primarily low-socioeconomic status students from diverse family backgrounds and Title I schools. The high-ability/gifted students consisted of three ethnically diverse subgroups of approximately equal size as the group of underserved students, including: (a) students of high average cognitive abilities (i.e., mean IQ approximately 110–120); (b) traditionally gifted students (i.e., mean IQ approximately 130), and (c) highly gifted students (i.e., mean IQ approximately 145). Students vary in class placement, ranging from "highly gifted centers" to clustering of gifted students within heterogeneous regular education placements.

Table 8.1 Goals

Goal	Student Outcome
Develop concepts related to understanding the world of science.	Provide examples and salient features of various concepts; classify various concepts; identify counterexamples of various concepts; create definitions or generalizations about various concepts.
Develop an understanding of the macroconcept of systems as applied to science content goals.	Identify the elements of a system; determine the boundaries of a system; label the inputs and the outputs of a system; analyze the system interactions.
Develop knowledge of selected content topics on botany.	Understand that plans have basic needs, including air, water, nutrients, and light; understand that different plant parts serve different functions in growth, survival, and reproduction; understand that plants undergo many changes during their life cycles; understand that different plants have different characteristics; understand that plants may cause changes in the environment where they live.
Develop interrelated science process skills.	Make observations; ask questions; learn more; design and conduct experiments; create meaning; tell others what was found.
Develop critical thinking skills.	Describe problematic situations or issues; define relevant concepts; identify different points of view in situations or issues; describe evidence or data supporting a scientific question; draw conclusions based on data (making inferences); predict consequences.
Develop creative thinking skills.	Develop fluency when naming objects and ideas, based on a stimulus; develop flexible thinking; elaborate on ideas presented in oral or written form; create novel products.
Develop curiosity and interest in the world of science.	Express reactions about discrepant events; ask meaningful questions about science topics; articulate ideas of interest about science; demonstrate persistence in completing science tasks.

What Are the Goals of the Project?

The goals of Project Clarion from a curricular and student learning perspective may best be seen in the a curriculum framework that delineates seven goals and related outcomes for each. As seen in Table 8.1, the project seeks to enhance conceptual understanding in science and beyond, to develop scientific reasoning abilities, and to instruct students in specific science topics of interest. A set of more generic goals includes an emphasis on critical and creative thinking and on scientific curiosity.

Project Curriculum

Project Clarion addressed the development of curiosity in science, critical and creative thinking, as well as the scientific research process and concept development related to systems and change. Problem-based learning was incorporated into each of the units, but was not the lead feature as in the earlier curriculum development work. Goals and student outcomes were aligned to the National Science Education Standards. Each lesson included instructions that provided the purpose, time needed, suggestions on how to implement the lesson, and ways to conclude and extend the exercise. Three sample units are described below to illustrate different grade levels and science domains addressed in the project.

Budding Botanists (Center for Gifted Education, 2009) is a life science unit for grades 1–2 with 13 lessons that engages students in a scenario-based approach to observe and investigate plant life. The macroconcept of systems guides students as they assume the role of botanists. Team members seek to understand the structure, nature, and life cycle of plants, and to answer questions such as "How can plants be used to fuel cars?" *Budding Botanists* received a 2008 NAGC Curriculum Studies Network award for outstanding curriculum and has been recommended by NSTA as a strong curriculum in science for young children.

Dig It! (Center for Gifted Education, 2010a) is an Earth and space science unit for third grade with 15 lessons that involves students in a problem-based approach to investigate humanity's effects on the environment, the importance of natural resources, and sound conservation practices. The macroconcept of change guides students as they assume the role of a preservation park planner. Team members examine examples of environmental pollution and conservation with hands-on scientific experiments and demonstrations.

Invitation to Invent (Center for Gifted Education, 2010b) is a physical science unit for grades 3–4 with 16 lessons that connects the scientific investigative process with creative problem solving. The macroconcept of systems guides students as they assume the role of inventor to solve an everyday problem using simple and complex machines. Students conduct investigations that support their learning about force, motion, and friction. Students also learn about the six simple machines and how they are put together to form more complex machines.

Research Design

In the 5-year, multidistrict Clarion studies, we used a quasi-experimental design to test the efficacy of the units in K–3 classrooms, using the Metropolitan Achievement Test (Prescott, Barlow, Hogan, & Farr, 2000), the Test of Critical Thinking (Bracken et al, 2004), and three performance-based measures to assess content, concept, and scientific research process skills as dependent variables. Comparison data were collected within other Title I schools in the same district. After 24 hours of instruction, posttests were administered to both groups. Analyses included multivariate analysis of variance (MANOVA).

Sample

The Clarion sample involved three school districts with 48 classrooms, of which 43 were controls. All experimental teachers received 3 days of training on implementing the units of study, 2 days before implementation began, and 1 day during the project implementation period. Additionally, each received an end-of-implementation debriefing opportunity in person with project staff.

Instruments

Project effectiveness in the Clarion study was also assessed on a revised form of the Fowler (1990) *Diet Cola Test*, which assesses students' application of scientific method and scientific reasoning skills. Additional instruments used in Project Clarion included two other project-developed, performance-based assessments, one standardized achievement measure (Metropolitan Achievement Test), and one critical thinking measure (Test of Critical Thinking).

Data Collection Procedures

Project staff collected data for Project Clarion at each school site between 2006 and 2008. These data included the pre- and postmeasures described previously, as well as fidelity of implementation data from teachers in the experimental group.

Data Analysis and Results

Posttest analyses were conducted using an analysis of covariance (ANCOVA) that covaried pretest, between-group differences. MANOVAs were conducted and effect sizes calculated. The Project Clarion results showed significant and important gains for all groups of Title I learners with respect to ability (gifted, average, low ability) and minority status (African American, Asian American, Hispanic American) across 2 years of data collection on all measures employed. Effect sizes were in the moderate range (i.e., $d = .32$ to .56; Kim et al., 2011). The second and third year of data collection revealed growth on performance-based measures in content, scientific process, and concept development, with moderate effect sizes (i.e., $d = .32$ to .62). The scientific process assessment was administered to experimental and control students in the third year of data collection and showed significant differences for second graders, but not for third graders in science process skills or in science content on the MAT (Bland, Chandler, Coxon, & VanTassel-Baska, 2010).

Challenges

The following areas of concern and issues all relate to the real-world application of packaged curriculum in schools. Because the culture of schools still vests the responsibility for the curriculum transmission process (from choice of material, to processes used to teach it, to follow-up approaches to assess its effectiveness) with the classroom teacher, there are many problems that arise in trying to achieve standardized use. Moreover, in the current climate of schools, it is difficult to innovate, as many principals already have narrowed the focus of teaching to a few emphases within a subject and grade level. The following concerns emerged to project staff as the most problematic and worthy of problem solution strategies.

Teacher preparation. Most of the teachers in the program needed greater background knowledge in science content and a comfort level with teaching it that they did not possess. They also did not have experience working with gifted students or using flexible management approaches in teaching them, including constructivist models such as problem-based learning. Teachers in this project expressed a lack of comfort with the science content, science concepts, and related pedagogy.

Flexibility in classroom and school organization to accommodate student experimentation. Neither the schools nor the classrooms involved in the project exhibited sufficient flexibility in implementing innovation. Most employed rigid pacing guides, management techniques, and prescriptive approaches to curriculum and assessment that hampered faithful implementation of a new project.

Attitudes of school personnel in low-income settings. The value system of many of the personnel in these schools placed so much emphasis on reading skills that other subjects, like science, received limited attention. Moreover, the high-stakes state test was viewed as the only relevant tool to assess student learning; regardless of the demonstration of other learning gains, this one instrument carried the most impact in educator thinking. Because science was tested at only one grade level in which the project was implemented, there was little room to make inferences about the impact of the project through such a measure. This project required teachers to provide 45 minutes of science instruction for 15 consecutive days; given their typical schedule of teaching science only twice a week for 30 minutes each time, teachers felt stressed by the demands of the grant relative to district and state requirements.

Lack of valuing research in practical settings. Collecting research data is a major obstacle in school settings in which research is not valued. Even with the provision of weekly assistance in the form of an "ambassador" to support teachers, and support for administering, collecting, and scoring assessments, this project proved to be very challenging. Often data were missing, teachers confused the pre- and posttests, and assessments sometimes were not administered at all due to time constraints.

Fidelity of implementation. As in Project Athena, a major problem that plagued Project Clarion across its pilot sites and years of operation was fidelity of implementation. Issues of teacher autonomy, administrator-driven initiatives, and time constraints resulted in a lack of fidelity of implementation.

Principal support for teacher experimentation. Although the principals in the project had indicated their support, they often neglected to emphasize the importance of its implementation across the 3 years. Programs emphasizing student learning in reading and math received more attention, to the detriment of science instruction in general and of the project specifically. Because Project Clarion was implemented in Title I schools, the principals had to manage multiple innovations, often giving this program little or no emphasis.

Contributions

The work of the Center for Gifted Education on Project Clarion provided several contributions to the field. In addition to new curriculum, other products included the construction of performance-based assessments relevant to the goals and outcomes of the project, professional development modules that prepare educators to implement the program effectively, and research studies that demonstrate student achievement gains.

Project Clarion has provided new curriculum materials in science at K–3 levels for low-income promising learners that meet the intent of the new Next Generation Science Standards (NGSS) in content, scientific research processes, and concept dimensions. Very few materials exist that incorporate differentiation techniques for the gifted, align to the new standards, and are tailored for use with this special population of gifted learners.

The research-based nature of the program provides support for replication and continued use of the materials. Findings have consistently shown learning gains in content, scientific processes, and concept learning. Moreover, students showed heightened motivation and teachers reported doing science more often as a result of the project.

The infusion of problem-based learning into each unit of study provided a research-based strategy for teachers to incorporate into their science teaching at these levels of instruction. The opportunity for young children to be initiators of their own learning has been a special feature that enhanced interest and motivation to do science (Bland et al., 2010).

A scope and sequence of science learning was incorporated from grades K–3 in the units in three major domains of science—biological, physical, and Earth science—which provides a building block for ongoing science instruction. The conceptual approach of the units, building from basic general concepts (e.g., space, time) to basic science concepts (e.g., magnetism, cells) to overarching concepts (e.g., systems, change) provided young children a strong foundation for understanding their world.

The performance-based assessments (PBAs) that employ concept maps and concept tasks to determine learning are an innovative feature of these curriculum packages. The use of PBAs provided more authentic evidence of student learning at young ages and suggested that these students were capable of learning more advanced material in science than often thought possible.

Additionally, a new science attitude scale was developed to assess teacher attitudes toward teaching science and the impact of the curriculum on those attitudes. Results suggest that teachers were more positive about teaching science after implementing the project.

Professional development modules were developed that provide both teachers and administrators the training necessary to implement Project Clarion effectively. The seven modules focus on the structure of the program, its curriculum and assessments, the use of scientific research design, the teaching of concepts, the use of problem-based learning, and implementation features that include grouping, the use of centers, and setting up classrooms. Administrator training focuses on the ways the program interfaces with the new science standards (NGSS) and the essential components of building and district implementation.

Important Research Findings

Project Clarion results suggested a trajectory of learning gains on different dimensions of science learning as a result of exposure to the 24 hours of classroom instruction in science concepts, content, and process for students in Title I classrooms receiving the intervention. However, learning on the science achievement scale was less impressive in the third-year results, suggesting the need for an instrument with a stronger curricular-content match to the concept-based units.

Although enhanced student learning is the primary indicator of curriculum effectiveness, teachers' favorable subjective impressions about their experiences with materials and related instructional strategies are also important. Such experiences support teacher acceptance of the materials and contribute to sustained use over time. Teacher acceptance was evaluated using a questionnaire administered at the conclusion of the implementation process. Teacher evaluation outcomes supported the quality of the units with respect to benefits to learners, applicability to science standards, and ease of implementation (Stambaugh, Chandler, Bland, & VanTassel-Baska, 2013).

In Project Clarion, teachers also rated the units of study individually, with project staff using the results to guide final revisions of the units. Focus groups were also employed to evaluate training and unit implementation; results suggested that the experience was helpful and illuminated what Title I students could do if given the opportunity to be actively engaged in a high-quality science curriculum.

Project Clarion has produced important findings that relate to several areas of interest. Student learning gains have been strong, with students demonstrating improvement in critical thinking, science achievement increases, and science concept learning gains. Using quasi-experimental designs, the project has demonstrated significant and important learning gains in these dimensions with effect sizes ranging from .3–.6 (Kim et al., 2011). Additionally, teachers have demonstrated learning gains in using differentiation strategies in key areas that include critical thinking, creative thinking, and accommodation for individual differences.

In addition, the project revealed important issues associated with administering programs for promising children at the primary levels of instruction in science (VanTassel-Baska et al., in press). The most important of these findings are as follows:

* K–1 students require more individualized and tailored assessments in order to determine their readiness levels to do science and to document the nature and extent of gains. Only by grade 2 are more conventional assessment administrations possible.

* This was the first science program that many of these students encountered in school, suggesting that science is not being formally taught in many settings at the K–2 levels.

* Teachers at early primary levels were slow to use grouping techniques, which hampered the engagement of students in actual experimentation. Too often they did demonstration lessons and asked students to respond.

* School support for science at these levels was not as strong as anticipated. Reading and math are more highly supported as subject areas as seen in pacing guides, instructional time allocations, and professional development opportunities at the school and district levels.

* In general, schools did not continue the program after funding ended. Rather, they moved into new programs for which additional external funding was available. This was prevalent despite strong learning gains for their students.

* The use of learning centers at the primary level in Title 1 schools is not the norm. Thus, approaches to more individualized instruction are severely hampered.
* These programs need internal coordination at the district level in order to be sustained. The one district that has continued to implement the program without external funding over the last 4 years has done so because of a strong leader in gifted education who advocates for low-income learners and works with principals to provide opportunities for these learners districtwide. This district is also one of the largest in the country, suggesting that size may favor the institutionalization of such programs through diffusion to new sites.
* Teachers at the primary level are less ready to do science with their students than at other grade levels and than in other subject areas. Often, the teachers had not taught science as a subject at the primary level. Many teachers in the project needed ongoing weekly support to engage in the use of the units of study. Assistance required included setting up of materials and labs, having lessons modeled, coteaching selected lessons, and assisting with the administration and scoring of assessments.

Program Maintenance

The program has run on a self-sustaining basis for the past 4 years and has been expanded to new districts during that time on the same model. Cost savings approaches have been used that use existing personnel but include a fee for professional development services through the Center for Gifted Education and fees for materials, procured directly from the publishing company. All author proceeds from the sale of materials (15%) go to a Center for Gifted Education fund to provide scholarships to graduate students who will work in curriculum development for the gifted.

School districts sustain the program by allocating funds to purchase materials and provide professional development to teachers. Usually this funding comes from ongoing operational budgets within the school district and/or the school. Replications of Project Clarion are occurring in several districts nationwide. One of the original districts also has incorporated Project Clarion into its Young Scholars' program for low-income and minority students at nine new school sites.

The curriculum from Project Clarion has also been used in two subsequent Javits projects at the University of Arkansas at Little Rock and Western Kentucky University. Findings from both projects have shown student learning gains and teacher motivation to provide ongoing science instruction in the form of Clarion units of study.

Contact Information

Contact regarding Project Clarion should be addressed to the Center for Gifted Education, PO Box 8795, College of William and Mary, Williamsburg, VA 23187.

The work reported herein was supported by the U. S. Department of Education, Jacob K., Javits Gifted and Talented Students Program under Award Number S206A0040059. The opinions, conclusions, and recommendations expressed in this chapter are those of the author and do not necessarily reflect the position or policies of the U.S. Department of Education.

References

Bland, L., Chandler, K., Coxon, S. & VanTassel-Baska, J. (2010). Science in the city. *Gifted Child Today, 33,* 48–57.

Bracken, B. Bai, W., Fithian, E., Lamprecht, B., Little, C., & Quek, C. (2004). *The Test of Critical Thinking.* Williamsburg, VA: Center for Gifted Education.

Center for Gifted Education. (2009). *Budding botanists*. Waco, TX: Prufrock Press.

Center for Gifted Education. (2010a). *Dig it!* Waco, TX: Prufrock Press.

Center for Gifted Education. (2010b). *Invention to invent*. Waco, TX: Prufrock Press.

Fowler, M. (1990). *The diet cola test. Science Scope, 13*, 32–34.

Kim, K. H., VanTassel-Baska, J., Bracken, B. A., Feng, A., Stambaugh, T., & Bland, L. (2011). Project Clarion: Three years of science instruction in Title I schools among K–third-grade students. *Research in Science Education, 42*, 813–829.

National Science Board. (2010). *Preparing the next generation of STEM innovators*. Washington, DC: Author.

Prescott, G. A., Barlow, I., Hogan, T., & Farr, R. C. (2000). *Metropolitan Achievement Test* (8th ed.). Minneapolis, MN: Pearson Assessments.

Stambaugh, T., Chandler, K., Bland, L., & VanTassel-Baska, J. (2013). *Implementing science innovation in the primary grades: Case study research*. Manuscript in preparation.

VanTassel-Baska, J., Bland, L., Stambaugh, T., Kim, K., Bracken, B., & Feng, A. (in press). Assessing science reasoning and conceptual understanding in the primary grades using multiple measures of performance: Project Clarion. *Journal of Advanced Academics*.

VanTassel-Baska, J. (2010). (Ed.). *Patterns and profiles of low-income gifted learners*. Waco, TX: Prufrock Press.

Conclusion

The No Child Left Behind Act (NCLB; 2001) as well as other local, state, and federal legislation focus on raising the academic achievement of students who are struggling learners. This is certainly a worthy and important goal, but there is evidence that although extra resources and personnel were provided in abundance for struggling learners, students with gifts and talents were not considered in the provisions (Plucker, Burroughs, & Song, 2010). Moreover, the Jacob K. Javits Gifted and Talented Programming Grant Program (Javits Grants), after nearly 20 years of providing funding for projects aimed at identifying and serving gifted and talented students from underserved populations, was eliminated from the federal budget in April 2011. Thus, at this time, there is no federal money earmarked for gifted and talented students.

The programs and program models in the previous chapters exemplify the work that has been done on behalf of gifted and talented students. Some were funded through Javits grants; others received private or public funding. All projects focus on target students from diverse populations in an effort to combat issues of high poverty and underrepresentation; these are the students who are most at risk for not being identified and served in programs for gifted and talented students.

Olszewski and Clarenbach (2012) provided seven barriers to participation of low-income, high-ability students in advanced programs:

* a conception of giftedness that emphasizes only already developed talent,
* misconceptions about low-income promising learners,
* pedagogy and curriculum that fails to support talent development,
* school identification policies,
* gifted program policies that hinder participation and performance,
* labeling students as "gifted," and
* lack of access to supplemental programs. (pp. 9–11)

By providing support and programming that aims to overcome these barriers, each of the programs and models represented in the previous chapters prepares students for advanced programs, advanced courses, and other opportunities in which they might not ordinarily enroll or for which they might not otherwise have been selected. Table C. 1 compares the programs and models across seven dimensions to provide a graphic overview to assist you in choosing what might work in your own context. We hope that the information provided in this book will assist you as you create the best possible program for your students who are culturally, linguistically, and economically diverse and who are or have the potential to be gifted and talented.

Table C.1 Comparison of Programs and Program Models

Program	Type	Grade(s) served	Focus	Key Features	Target Population	Funding
Project Excite	Out-of-school enrichment	Grades 3–8	Math and science	Academic enrichment; parent education and support; supplemental programming and resources	African American and Latino students	University-school partnership
Project M³	In-school math replacement or enrichment units	Grades 3–5	Mathematics curriculum	Critical thinking; in-depth investigations; students work like practicing mathematicians	Disadvantaged backgrounds	Javits Grant
Next Generation Venture Fund	In-school and out-of-school support	Grades 8–12	Scholarship program to allow students from target population to enter selective colleges	Scholastic, personal, and social support to students beginning in eighth grade and continuing through high school graduation; Students and parents sign a contract to participate	Academically talented African American, Latino, and Native Americans of poverty	Goldman Sachs Foundation, primarily
Young Scholars Program K-2	In-school and out-of-school	Grades K-2	Early identification and service for low-income, high-ability students	Early identification of potential; identified students clustered with appropriate teachers; enrichment opportunities after school and in summer; parent support	Low-income students of potential	Funded by school district
The TEAK Fellowship	Out-of-school, year-round	Grades 7–12	Provides academic and personal support for talented students from low-income families	Students are accepted as sixth graders; participate in afterschool, Saturday, and summer programs, and internships; provides support for high school search and placement; regular communication; mentoring; college guidance; parent support	High poverty; New York City only	Privately funded, by individual, foundation, and corporate donors
Project NEXUS	Grants to high poverty schools in Maryland	Middle and high schools	Grants to schools to extend opportunities for students from low income to gain access to challenging college prep coursework	Professional development for teachers and counselors focused on AP and pre-AP; curriculum vertical alignment; partnerships that offer career days, field trips, college planning	High poverty	Federal Advanced Placement Incentive Program

Table C.1, Continued

Program	Type	Grade(s) served	Focus	Key Features	Target Population	Funding
Project Athena	Grades 3-5	English Language Arts	ELA enrichment or replacement units	Professional development for teachers focused on higher level thinking skills; development of instrumentation sensitive to low-socioeconomic learners for identification and assessment of learning; implementation and refinement of research-based language arts curriculum units	Title I schools	Javits Grant
Project Clarion	Grades K–3	Science	Science enrichment or replacement units	Professional development for teachers focused on science content and concepts; use of instrumentation sensitive to low-socioeconomic learners for identification and assessment of learning; development and implementation of research-based science concept curriculum in grades K–3.	Title I schools	Javits Grant

References

No Child Left Behind Act of 2001. Public Law 97–110, 20 U.S.C. Section 6301.

Olszewski-Kubilius, P., & Clarenbach, J. (2012). *Unlocking emergent talent: Supporting high achievement of low-income, high-ability students.* Washington, DC: National Association for Gifted Children.

Plucker, J. A., Burroughs, N., & Song, R. (2010). *Mind the (other) gap! The growing excellence gap in K–12 education.* Bloomington: Indiana University, Center for Evaluation & Education Policy.

Appendices

Appendix A

Project M³ Student Profile

Date: _____ School: _____

Name of Student: _____

Name of Teacher: _____

Instructions: Please complete this form for the top one-half of the students in your class. Read each item in the scale and place an "X" in the box that corresponds with the frequency you have observed the behavior.

Scoring:
a) Add the total number of X's in each column to obtain the "Column Total."
b) Multiply the "Column Total" by the "Weight" to obtain the "Weighted Column Total."
c) Sum the "Weighted Column Totals" across to obtain the Total Score.

MATHEMATICS CHARACTERISTICS[1]
© 2003 M. Katherine Gavin

The student...	Never	Very Rarely	Rarely	Occasionally	Frequently	Always
1. is eager to solve challenging math problems (A problem is defined as a task for which the solution is not known in advance).	☐	☐	☐	☐	☐	☐
2. organizes data and information to discover mathematical patterns.	☐	☐	☐	☐	☐	☐
3. enjoys challenging math puzzles, games, and logic problems.	☐	☐	☐	☐	☐	☐
4. understands new math concepts and processes more easily than other students.	☐	☐	☐	☐	☐	☐
5. has creative (unusual and divergent) ways of solving math problems.	☐	☐	☐	☐	☐	☐
6. displays a strong number sense (e.g., makes sense of large and small numbers, estimates easily and appropriately).	☐	☐	☐	☐	☐	☐
7. frequently solves math problems abstractly, without the need for manipulatives or concrete materials	☐	☐	☐	☐	☐	☐
8. looks at the world from a mathematical perspective (e.g., notices spatial relationships, finds math patterns that are not obvious, is curious about quantitative information).	☐	☐	☐	☐	☐	☐
9. when solving a math problem, can switch strategies easily, if appropriate or necessary.	☐	☐	☐	☐	☐	☐
10. regularly uses a variety of representations to explain math concepts (written explanations, pictorial, graphic, equations, etc.)	☐	☐	☐	☐	☐	☐
Add Column Total						
Multiply by Weight	×1	×2	×3	×4	×5	×6
Add Weight Column Totals						
Scale Total						

Mathematics Characteristics is based on the work of Dr. Joseph S. Renzulli's *Scales for Rating the Behavioral Characteristics of Superior Students*, © 2002, Prufrock Press, Waco, TX. http://www.prufrock.com. Used with permission.

	Level 3	Level 4	Level 5
Number and Operators	Unraveling the Mystery of the MoLi Stone: Place Value and Numeration	Factors, Multiples and Leftovers: Linking Multiplication and Division	Treasures From the Attic: Exploring Fractions
Algebra	Awesome Algebra: Looking for Patterns and Generalizations	At the Mall With Algebra: Working With Variables and Equations	Record Makers and Breakers: Using Algebra to Analyze Change
Geometry and Measurement	What's the *Me* in *Measurement* All About?	Getting Into Shapes	Funkytown Fun House: Focusing on Proportional Reasoning and Similarity
Data Analysis and Probability	Digging for Data: The Search Within Research	Analyze This! Representing and Interpreting Data	What Are Your Chances?

Figure 2.1. Project M³ unit description.

Rules for Odd or Even

Number of Players: 2; Player E and Player O

Each player spins one of the spinners at the same time. The results are added to find the sum. If the sum is even, Player E gets a point. If the sum is odd, Player O gets a point. Play 16 rounds and record your results. The player with the most points at the end of the rounds wins the game.

Figure 2.2. Game rules. From *What Are Your Chances?* by M. Katherine Gavin, Suzanne H. Chapin, Judith Daley, and Linda Sheffield, 2008, Dubuque, IA: Kendall Hunt. Copyright 2008 by Kendall Hunt. Reprinted with permission.

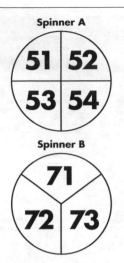

Figure 2.3. Spinners. From *What Are Your Chances?* by M. Katherine Gavin, Suzanne H. Chapin, Judith Daley, and Linda Sheffield, 2008, Dubuque, IA: Kendall Hunt. Copyright 2008 by Kendall Hunt. Reprinted with permission.

Figure 2.4. Think Deeply question. From *What Are Your Chances?* by M. Katherine Gavin, Suzanne H. Chapin, Judith Daley, and Linda Sheffield, 2008, Dubuque, IA: Kendall Hunt. Copyright 2008 by Kendall Hunt. Reprinted with permission.

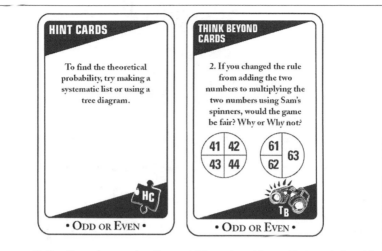

Figure 2.5. Sample cards. From *What Are Your Chances?* by M. Katherine Gavin, Suzanne H. Chapin, Judith Daley, and Linda Sheffield, 2008, Dubuque, IA: Kendall Hunt. Copyright 2008 by Kendall Hunt. Reprinted with permission.

Appendix B

Attachment 4-C

Student Name _____ Grade_____ Date_____

GIFTED BEHAVIORS RATING SCALE WITH COMMENTARY

A *Gifted Behaviors Rating Scale with Commentary (GBRSw/C)* is required for screening for full-time Advanced Academic Programs (AAP) Level IV placement.

Review each category and the list of descriptors. Assign an overall rating using the scale below.

Add the four scores and place the sum in the total box.

Behaviors Demonstrated:

1 = rarely

2 = occasionally   **TOTAL** [ ]

3 = frequently

4 = consistently

1. **Exceptional Ability to Learn**   [ ]
   - Exhibits exceptional memory
   - Demonstrates in-depth knowledge
   - Displays persistent, intense focus on one or more topics
   - Is highly reflective and/or sensitive to his/her environment
   - Learns and adapts readily to new cultures
   - Learns quickly and easily
   - Acquires language at a rapid pace
   - Learns skills independently and makes connections without formal instruction

2. **Exceptional Application of Knowledge**   [ ]
   - Demonstrates highly developed reasoning
   - Employs complex problem-solving strategies
   - Uses and interprets advanced symbol systems in academics, visual arts, and/or performing arts
   - Understands, applies, transfers abstract concepts
   - Uses technology in advanced applications
   - Acts as an interpreter, translator, and/or facilitator to help others
   - Makes advanced connections and transfers learning to other subjects, situations, cultures
   - Communicates learned concepts through role playing and/or detailed artwork

3. **Exceptional Creative/Productive Thinking**   [ ]
   - Sees the familiar in unusual ways / Does not conform to typical ways of thinking or perceiving
   - Is highly creative and/or inventive
   - Demonstrates unusual fluency and flexibility in thinking and problem-solving
   - Expresses ideas, feelings, experiences, and/or beliefs in original ways
   - Displays keen sense of humor
   - Is highly curious
   - Generates new ideas, new uses, new solutions easily
   - Perceives and manipulates patterns, colors, and/or symbols

4. **Exceptional Motivation to Succeed**   [ ]
   - Demonstrates ability to lead large and/or small groups
   - Meets exceptional personal and/or academic challenges
   - Explores, researches, questions topics, ideas, issues independently
   - Is poised with adults and engages them in adult conversations
   - Exhibits a strong sense of loyalty and responsibility
   - Demonstrates exceptional ability to adapt to new experiences
   - Strives to achieve high standards especially in areas of strength and/or interest
   - Shows initiative, self-direction, and/or high level of confidence

GBRS Rating completed by a school committee (FCPS)

From *Gifted Behaviors Rating Scale*, by B. Shaklee, 2002, Fairfax, VA: Fairfax County Public Schools. © 2002 by Fairfax County Public Schools. Reprinted with permission.

About the Editors

Cheryll M. Adams, Ph. D., is the Director Emerita of the Center for Gifted Studies and Talent Development at Ball State University and teaches graduate courses in research and gifted education. She has authored or coauthored numerous publications in professional journals, as well as several books and book chapters. She has coauthored and directed three Jacob K. Javits grants. She serves on the editorial review boards for *Roeper Review*, *Gifted Child Quarterly, Journal of Advanced Academics,* and *Journal for the Education of the Gifted.* She has served on the Board of Directors of the National Association for Gifted Children and has been president of the Indiana Association for the Gifted and of The Association for the Gifted, Council for Exceptional Children. She currently serves on the board of the Florida Association for the Gifted.

Kimberley L. Chandler, Ph.D., is the Curriculum Director at the Center for Gifted Education at the College of William and Mary and a Clinical Assistant Professor. Kimberley completed her Ph.D. in Educational Policy, Planning, and Leadership with an emphasis in gifted education administration at the College of William and Mary. Her professional background includes teach-

ing gifted students in a variety of settings, serving as an administrator of a school district gifted program, and providing professional
development training for teachers and administrators nationally and
internationally. Currently, Kimberley is the network representative on
the NAGC Board of Directors, member-at-large representative for
the AERA Research on Giftedness and Talent SIG, newsletter editor
of the CEC-TAG newsletter *The Update*, and an American delegate to
the World Council for Gifted and Talented Children. Her research
interests include curriculum policy and implementation issues in
gifted programs, the design and evaluation of professional development programs for teachers of the gifted, and the role of principals
in gifted education. Kimberley coauthored a book titled *Effective
Curriculum for Underserved Gifted Students* and has served as the editor
of many curriculum materials (science, social studies, language arts,
and mathematics) from the Center for Gifted Education.

About the Contributors

Kourtney Cockrell has managed the Project EXCITE program at the Center for Talent Development (CTD) for the past 3 1/2 years. Kourtney developed the EXCITE parent committee group, coordinated social and education programs for EXCITE families, and established a number of partnerships that expanded access for students and parents. She is currently pursuing a Master's of Science in learning and organizational change at the School of Education and Social Policy at Northwestern University. Kourtney graduated from the University of Michigan with degrees in Afroamerican and African Studies and Sociology.

Katherine Gavin, Ph.D., is an associate professor at the Neag Center for Gifted Education and Talent Development at the University of Connecticut. The main focus of her research is the development and evaluation of advanced math curriculum for elementary students. Dr. Gavin received the 2006 National Association for Gifted Children Early Leader award and the 2012 Neag School of Education Distinguished Researcher Award from the University of Connecticut. She has published over 100 articles, book chapters, and curriculum materials on mathematics education with a focus on gifted students. She has over 30 years experience in education as a math teacher, curriculum coordinator, math department chair, and assistant principal. She works with teachers nationally and internationally who are interested in developing mathematical thinking and talent in their students.

Renée C. Haston is currently the Director of the Next Generation Venture Fund (NGVF) for the Duke University Talent Identification Program, Northwestern Center for Talent Development, and the Center for Bright Kids. She is personally and professionally passionate about providing access for academically gifted students from underrepresented backgrounds. Through the NGVF program, she enjoys having the opportunity to enable students' acceptance into selective colleges and universities, which has allowed them to enter challenging careers and emerge as active leaders in society. Renée is a graduate of Duke University and James Madison University.

Carol V. Horn, Ph.D, is Coordinator of Advanced Academic Programs for Fairfax County Public Schools in northern Virginia and has worked in gifted education for over 25 years. Dr. Horn has a Master's of Education in educational psychology with an emphasis on gifted education from the University of Virginia and a doctorate in teacher preparation and special education from George Washington University. She is the 2002 recipient of the Hollingsworth Award from the National Association for Gifted Children for an outstanding research study in the field of gifted education, and in 2010, she received the first Outstanding Leader Award from the Center for Gifted Education at the College of William & Mary. Dr. Horn has worked extensively to develop and implement the Young Scholars model, a comprehensive approach to finding and nurturing advanced academic potential in young learners from underrepresented populations.

Katie Leh graduated from Pennsylvania State University in 2006, where she majored in marketing and minored in psychology. Katie joined The TEAK Fellowship in 2008, first as the Development & Alumni Associate and then as the Assistant Director of Communications & Development. She currently serves as a Communications & Development Consultant at TEAK.

Beth Onofry graduated from Dartmouth College in 2002, where she majored in psychology and minored in education. From 2002–2005, Beth recruited and evaluated prospective students and organized programming events as Assistant Director of Admissions and then Senior Assistant Director of Admissions at Dartmouth. Beth earned her Master's degree in learning and teaching in 2006 from Harvard University Graduate School of Education and later completed her Master's in School Counseling from Long Island University in 2009. Beth has worked at The TEAK Fellowship since 2006 as both Assistant Director of Post-Placement and Associate Director of Post-Placement, and currently serves as the Director of High School Programs at TEAK.

Jeanne L. Paynter, Ed.D, has led the development and implementation of Pre-K–12 gifted education policy and programming and professional development at the national, state, and local levels. Currently, Dr. Paynter is the State Specialist for gifted and talented education at the Maryland State Department of Education (MSDE), where she was instrumental in the development of new state policies in gifted programming and teacher certification. Dr. Paynter was Project Director for numerous USDOE grants to increase the participation and performance of low-income students in advanced-level courses. She led the development of the MSDE Primary Talent Development Early Learning Program, targeting the identification of non-mainstream gifted students. Dr. Paynter is a passionate advocate for gifted children and has authored book chapters, articles, and presentations for parent advocates. Dr. Paynter earned a B.S. in English from the Towson University, and her M.S. in gifted education and doctorate in teacher development and leadership from Johns Hopkins University.

Joyce VanTassel-Baska, Ed.D., is the Smith Professor Emerita of Education and founding director of the Center for Gifted Education at The College of William and Mary, where she developed a graduate program and a research and development center in gifted education. Formerly, she initiated and directed the Center for Talent Development at Northwestern University. She has also served as the state director of gifted programs for Illinois, as a regional director of a gifted service center in the Chicago area, as coordinator of gifted programs for the Toledo, OH, public school system, and as a teacher of gifted high school students in English and Latin. Dr. VanTassel-Baska has published widely, including 28 books and over 550 referenced journal articles, book chapters, and scholarly reports. Her major research interests are the talent development process and effective curricular interventions with the gifted.